P9-DJA-474

CHILDREN OF DIVORCE:

A Developmental Approach
to
Residence and Visitation

Mitchell A. Baris, Ph.D.
Carla B. Garrity, Ph.D.

Copyright © 1988 Psytec

All rights reserved. No part of this book may be reproduced by any process, electronic or mechancial, including photocopy, audio and/or visual recording, duplication in an informational storage and retrieval system, without written permission of the Publisher. Printed by Blue Ridge Printing Company, Inc., Asheville, NC. Published by Psytec Corporation, P.O. Box 564, DeKalb, IL 60115.

Library of Congress Catalog Card Number: 87-63449
ISBN: 0-940929-06-6

ACKNOWLEDGMENTS

We would like to thank our spouses, friends and colleagues who assisted us in the preparation of this book, especially Randy Sue Baris, Deena Raffe, and Sandra Rush.

TABLE OF CONTENTS

Preface

Through the years, parents have come to our psychology practices asking for child development knowledge that can be used when making custody and visitation decisions for the benefit of their children. This book is designed to address this need.

As psychologists, we recognize that every factor in the lives of parents and children, and within the dynamics of their relationships, may be a factor worthy of consideration in the determination of a sound post-separation residence and visitation arrangement. This book, therefore, risks being an oversimplification of an overwhelmingly complex issue.

Parents, we believe, are in the best position to understand their own children, their subtleties, desires, their unique reactions and means of expression. We feel that parents should make the basic decisions regarding their children's well being; relying on outsiders, mental health experts, and judges as a last resort. In the research (Steinman, Zemmelman, & Knoblauch, 1985) and in our practices, we have found that parents who make their own decisions about residence and visitation issues report greater satisfaction with and commitment to the arrangements. The healing process following a divorce is delayed for parents who have gone through lengthy court battles. These parents report feelings of lingering bitterness, manifested by heightened animosities, distrust, and grossly disrupted communication.

This divorce-related material is presented from the frequently overlooked point of view of the child. Necessarily, parents may feel slighted; their needs are not addressed in this book. This book is written in your children's best interests. Their needs are considered as equal to if not more important than your own. Meeting relationship needs in childhood is critical for the establishment of healthy relationships throughout adulthood. Children, who had no decision-making input into their own residence and visitation arrangements when their parents chose to separate, regardless experience the pain and outrage of the ensuing readjustment difficulties. There are many decisions parents can make to minimize the long-range psychological consequences of divorce on their children. This book is for those parents who want to make responsible decisions concerning residence and visitation arrangements for their children and seek to understand the psychological and developmental foundations upon which professionals base their recommendations.

The aim of this book is to temper with knowledge the judgments made by parents. The factual and conceptual information presented herein has been garnered from research findings put forth in the areas of child development and divorce, as well as from our experiences, successes and failures, in child and family therapy. We have also functioned as custody mediators, and as evaluators and expert witnesses on behalf of children who are the objects and often the victims of family litigation. Our specific guidelines for residence and visitation arrangements have evolved from this knowledge base.

Introduction

Forty years ago, couples stayed together for the sake of their children, and divorce not only engendered personal feelings of guilt but reactions of shame and embarrassment. Divorce was achieved at a semi-public airing of one's personal and marital failures where courts assigned blame and one parent was determined to be at fault.

The early seventies ushered in a new concept of family. Divorce became easier to obtain and more couples sought divorce as a solution when conflict arose. The myth proliferated that children were resilient, that if parents felt fulfilled in pursuing what they felt were their individual goals, then the children, in turn, would benefit from the parents' overall improvement. In essence, the "me" generation philosophy was introduced into the family. Thus, the new adage was "don't stay together for the sake of the children." Being divorced was no longer a shame or embarrassment; divorce was an acceptable solution to disappointment or conflict with one's spouse or even a wish for more personal fulfillment.

As more men and women struggled through the anguish of rebuilding their lives, self-help books appeared legitimizing divorce, telling how to get divorced without an attorney, how to negotiate finances, and how not to worry about the children. Books and articles appeared for children suggesting that divorce was just another meaning of family, overlooking the dismay, confusion, and feelings of loss with which children of divorce are left to struggle. Thus the notion evolved that "everyone's doing it and the children will adjust."

Today the statistics are staggering: 60% of all two year olds will end up in a single-parent family before age 18 (*U.S. News and World Report,* October 27, 1986). What kind of adults will these children become? How important is it to grow up with a mom and a dad who live together in the same household? What kind of marriage relationships will these children of divorce establish for themselves? Will these children choose more wisely because of their own experi-

ences? The answers are only beginning to appear as the children of
the early seventies are reaching adulthood and forming their own
families.

As answers emerge, the myth of children's resiliency is gradually falling away. Children do not "weather the storm" as successfully as parents and professionals may have expected. The after-
math may be long and anguishing; the legacy may be carried into
adulthood. Children of divorce, grown into adulthood, often report
sadness and pain in reflecting back on their childhood experiences;
they feel cheated out of growing up in an intact family; and they
generally do less well psychologically, socially and educationally
than children from intact families (Wallerstein, 1985). After inter-
viewing grown children aged nineteen to twenty-nine, ten years
following their parents' divorces, Judith Wallerstein (1985) states,
"A significant number are burdened by vivid memories of the
unhappy events at the time of the marital rupture. Their predominant feelings as they look backward are restrained sadness, some
remaining resentment at their parents, and a wistful sense of
having missed out on the experiences of growing up in an intact
family." These same young people carry into adulthood a concept of
themselves as "children of divorce" and many cite the demise of
their families as the most significant event of their lives. Research
(Kalter, Riemer, Brickman, & Chen, 1985) now shows that children,
especially girls, who may appear to have adjusted to a divorce in
childhood could have a "time bomb like" reaction and may begin
troublesome sexual activity, drug use, and running away during the
adolescent years.

Many psychological patterns seem to perpetuate from generation to generation. Most of us, without great effort to do otherwise,
parent the way we were parented and create families that are
similar to the ones in which we grew up. The children of divorce
have not all grown into adulthood yet. Will they have the capacity
to build long-lasting and emotionally satisfying relationships, or
will they be left with psychological scars that prevent such relationship building, leaving them to reflect at the end of their own
lives on what may not have been there for them?

No one can undo all of the consequences of growing up too soon
or growing up without the feeling of a protective nest to return to in
times of stress and life changes. As adults, each of us must weigh
our personal circumstances and reasons for seeking a divorce. Some

situations are intolerable. Each person is unique in what he/she can tolerate and cope with in the way of marital conflict.

This book is for parents who are seeking a separation or divorce or have done so in the past. THIS INFORMATION IS NOT RECOMMENDED FOR EVERYONE. The parents for whom this book is recommended are:

1. Those parents who are bonded to their children, i.e., those who actively have parented their children up until the time of the parental separation.
2. Those parents with competent parenting skills, where children are not in physical or psychological danger at either parent's home.
3. Those parents who are available and willing to parent the children and when required, will put their children's needs ahead of their own.

This book is not for those parents who must win at all costs, nor for those who cannot put their own needs aside to allow their children to be "the winners." Neither is this book for those who would manipulate their children to win vindication against the other parent who may have hurt them. Additionally, this book is not recommended for those parents who cannot relinquish any of the parenting role due to the fear of perceived or imagined societal or familial condemnation. And last, it is definitely not for those parents who represent a threat of physical harm to the children due to impaired judgment from use of drugs, alcohol, or from other emotional or behavioral disorders.

Guiding Principles

In seeking to make decisions about residence and visitation for the ultimate benefit of the children, there are three basic guidelines to follow:

1. Minimize loss.
2. Maximize the relationship with each parent.
3. Allow the successful mastery of age appropriate developmental tasks and consider redesigning arrangements for each child as development progresses.

Of course, these guidelines must be applied with flexibility and common sense.

1. Minimize loss.

Divorce, in almost all cases, represents loss to a child. In its more extreme form, the loss can include complete abandonment by one parent, uprooting from friends, extended family, school, and community, moves to geographically unfamiliar locations, and a slide from financial well-being to economic impoverishment.

Most ideally, but too infrequently, divorce can result in a minimal loss. Where both mom and dad remain in close proximity, the children can have easy and open access to each of the parents.

When formulating decisions and plans, attempt to minimize losses whenever possible. For example, if it is not an economic necessity, do not sell the house this year; if a move must take place, move to less expensive housing in the same neighborhood and school district. Additionally, maintain contacts with the children's friends and maximize contacts with individuals in the extended support system such as grandparents, aunts, uncles, cousins and family friends.

2. Maximize the relationship with each parent.

This book is oriented toward the ultimate establishment of a sense of family where the children feel they have reasonable and comfortable access to each parent in his or her new family situation. This means a time sharing arrangement which suits the needs of the children and the availability of the parents, possibly fifty-fifty, possibly not. Varieties of such arrangements are described in Isolina Ricci's (1980) book, *Mom's House, Dad's House.* As a guiding principle, it is safer to decide in favor of what research has established to be known in the field. Many alternative arrangements may appear to be working for a period of time but the long- range effects are as yet unknown. The recommendations throughout this book are based on what is known about the needs of children.

In the area of attachment, it is the parent who has had less involvement in the physical care of the child who needs to be patient. While the ultimate goal is to maximize the relationship with each parent, it is important to move gradually into time-sharing parenting arrangements for young children. There is a lifetime of parenting, relating and enjoying ahead. There is no need to rush into a fifty-fifty split arrangement too quickly because doing so can cause more harm than benefit in the long run. This concept is explored further in the developmental chapters.

3. Allow the successful mastery of age appropriate development tasks and consider redesigning arrangements for each child as development progresses.

While development is an on-going process, certain tasks take on predominance at different stages of development. Trauma, stress, or difficult circumstances at a given age can interfere with the mastery of the primary tasks of that age. Developmental tasks that have not been mastered may accumulate and have a potentially negative impact on later development. Eventually, satisfactory and healthy emotional development will not proceed further, and professional intervention may be required for remediation. These developmental tasks, which are prominent at different stages of development, play a crucial role in guiding living arrangements and visitation recommendations.

Because development is an on-going process, it is important to determine residence and visitation by developmental age. Although there is individual variation, most children's developmental needs change within an age frame of two and a half to three years. This means that approximately every two to three years the arrangements may become antiquated and need to be revised. As a rule of thumb, it is important for parents to maintain open lines of communication with each other and to consider appropriate revisions in residence and visitation arrangements as children's unique needs change during the maturing process.

Joint Versus Sole Custody

Joint custody is a confusing concept. Legally, the term denotes an arrangement by which parents share jointly in major decisions affecting their child, in areas such as schooling, medical attention, religion, and other decisions. Joint custody does not mean, however, that the parents must split the living arrangements fifty-fifty. Until recently, the courts rarely assisted parents in deciding what the living arrangements and the visitation patterns should be. Now a distinction is being made between "joint legal custody" and "joint physical custody." Joint legal custody refers to shared decision making power while joint physical custody refers to shared residences. In a joint physical custody arrangement, the children alternate between the mother's residence and the father's residence. Still this does not mean that the children must divide their time equally between the two homes, unless specifically mandated by the court. Parents with joint physical custody arrangements are otherwise free to adopt any living arrangements they wish, provided mother, father, and the children are content with the decision.

Regardless of the legal custody arrangement, it is necessary from a psychological standpoint to modify custody and visitation agreements as children mature. Often the court has awarded custody to one parent and outlined a visitation arrangement for the other parent. When this is the case, parents wishing to modify their current arrangements are advised to check with their attorneys regarding the laws in their area. Thus, the guidelines presented in this book are for all parents regardless of their legal custody arrangements and are designed to assist parents in planning for their children according to their developmental needs.

Joint custody is not a psychological concept. Shared parenting, however, is important psychologically. Wallerstein and Kelly (1980) found that parents who are not involved in ongoing decision making for their children tend to slowly drop out of their children's lives. This gradual loss of a parent is likely to place a heavy emotional burden on children.

As a prerequisite for effective parenting after divorce, it is important to apply these guidelines with flexibility and common sense. Rather than rigidly attempting to apply the principles set forth here to a particular situation, you need to be open to mitigating circumstances (i.e., siblings, handicaps, geographic distance, etc.) that make your children's situations unique and to tailor the principles accordingly. Appendix A outlines a sample parenting agreement which can be individualized to your children's needs.

Overview

The chapters that follow this introduction are laid out in sequence, detailing developmental tasks for each age level. Included in each chapter is a discussion of the risks at stake for failing to allow satisfactory mastery of developmental tasks. There are descriptions of typical age-related problem behaviors which may be brought on by parental separation and divorce. Finally, residence and visitation arrangements geared to each developmental stage are presented. For easy reference, these guidelines are offered in chart form prior to the developmental chapters of the book. The developmental chapters will assist in interpreting and utilizing the charts.

DEVELOPMENTAL GUIDELINES
FOR
RESIDENCE AND VISITATION
ARRANGEMENTS

Infancy to Two and a Half Years

Developmental Guidelines For Residence and Visitation Arrangements

Developmental Tasks	Child's Divorce Issues	Recommendations: Parents Living Close to Each Other	Recommendations: Parents Living Far Apart	Risks
Infants Build attachment to primary caretaker Form trust in the environment Toddlers Begin to develop a sense of independence Increased self awareness assisted by emergence of language and locomotion Growing capacity to use symbols for comforting self	Feeling of loss of contact with primary caretaking parent Feeling of loss of familiar and comfortable environment	Select primary residence based on caretaking history Non-residential parent has short, frequent visits daily depending on availability and caretaking history If dual primary parents, share daytime caretaking, establish one nighttime caretaker Overnights are not recommended	One parent travels to the residence of the other to enable non-residential parent to have daily short visitation Maintain long-distance relationship (see Appendix C)	Feeling of loss of contact with primary parent results in symptoms of depression and regression (acting younger) Too long a separation from primary caretaker may result in problems with separation and relationship capacity in later stages of development

Two and a Half to Five Years

Developmental Guidelines For Residence and Visitation Arrangements

Developmental Tasks	Child's Divorce Issues	Recommendations: Parents Living Close to Each Other	Recommendations: Parents Living Far Apart	Risks
Continued growth of individuality	Magical thinking resulting in sense of responsibility for divorce	Time initially distributed in proportion to parent's direct caretaking prior to divorce	One parent travels to the residence area of the other	Losing mastery of developmental tasks previously mastered
Capacity to hold absent parent in mind to comfort self for extended periods	Anxiety around basic needs being met—feeding, shelter, visitation logistics, and abandonment	May introduce longer visitation periods for child gradually throughout this stage to a maximum of a split week	Child overnights—2 to 3 days maximum	Loss of opposite-sex parent as socialization agent or loss of same-sex parent as identification model
Verbal skills develop for expression of feelings and needs	Fantasizes intact family and denies divorce	Implement overnights for child—1 per week initially, extend to a maximum of 3 per week toward the end of this stage	Must have encouragement and help to maintain essential phone and letter contact with absent parent between visits	Experiencing feelings of abandonment may result in sadness, depression, low self-esteem, and interference with development
Regulation and mastery of emotions and bodily functions	Fantasies and actions relating to reuniting of parents	Long-weekend, short-weekend concept, preferably including a weekday visit, is a possibility if one parent works full time during the week and the other does not	Carry photographs, transitional objects, and memorabilia of absent parent	Carrying power struggles characteristic of this age to later phases of development
Increasing identification with same-sex parent	Transition difficulties in moving between households can be expected			

Six to Eight Years

Developmental Guidelines For Residence and Visitation Arrangements

Developmental Tasks	Child's Divorce Issues	Recommendations: Parents Living Close to Each Other	Recommendations: Parents Living Far Apart	Risks
Developing peer and community relationships	Prevailing sadness	Many children still require a home base	With history of attachment and involvement with out-of-state parent, child can phase in travel alone for up to two week-long visits (summer, Christmas and spring break)	Achievement at school and learning affected
Moral development	Direct expression of pain and anger	Child visits from 1 to 3 days weekly with non-residential parent		Long-term depression
Empathy, greater internal regulation of impulses	Fears around money, food, and a place to live	OR	Distant parent may have frequent week-long visits, including overnights, in the geographic area of the child's primary residence area if parents' finances and work schedules permit. During these visits maintain the child's consistent contact with community, peer group, school and extracurricular activities	Preoccupation with divorce
Self-concept development around competence and mastery	Fear of losing both parents	Alternating half weeks at each parent's home if consistent contact with community, peer group, school and extracurricular activities can be maintained		Acting out around theme of parents reuniting
	Self blame manifested by feelings of responsibility and attempts to reunite parents	Child could have multiple overnights	Child must have permission and help to maintain essential phone and letter contact with absent parent between visits	
		Full week at each parent's home can be phased in toward older end of this stage	Visits may be longer (up to 4 weeks) toward older end of stage or if accompanying older sibling and formerly very involved non-residential parent, especially if children are visiting an area in which they have previously resided	
			Homesickness possible. May need to curtail lengthy visits	

Nine to Twelve Years

Developmental Guidelines For Residence and Visitation Arrangements

Developmental Tasks	Child's Divorce Issues	Recommendations: Parents Living Close to Each Other	Recommendations: Parents Living Far Apart	Risks
Proficiency in skill areas: academic, athletic, artistic, community activity	Empathic understanding of one or both parents with possible intense condemnation for one parent	One home base with specific evenings, weekends, and activities at the other home scheduled for regularity and predictability	One home base with one to three weekend visits per month at other home, depending on distance and capacity to travel	Academic interference
Developing an increased awareness of self, evaluating own strengths and weaknesses as compared to others	Demanding adequate adult-level explanations	OR	Non-residential parent will travel to home base to involve self with teachers, instructors, to attend performances and important events	Possible lying or other deceptive behavior
Fitting in to the peer-level social order	Aware of own rejection and vulnerability; obvious and sustained feelings of sadness, anger and hurt	Equal basis with each parent is possible, up to 2 weeks in each residence	Half of Christmas break, all of spring break with non-residential parent	Forming too close an alliance with one parent against the other
	Possible sense of shame in community	Maintain accessibility to school, peers, extracurricular and community involvements from both homes	If too far for regular weekends, then Thanksgiving and Presidents' Day weekend with non-residential parent	Loneliness, depression, low self-esteem
		"Nesting": both parents moving in and out of same residence is another possibility	Presuming close relationship exists, summers may be split 50-50, approximately 4 to 6 weeks in one block	
		Presuming close relationship, summers may be split 50-50 approximately 4 to 6 weeks in one block		

Thirteen to Eighteen Years

Developmental Guidelines For Residence and Visitation Arrangements

Developmental Tasks	Child's Divorce Issues	Recommendations: Parents Living Close to Each Other	Recommendations: Parents Living Far Apart	Risks
Psychological emancipation: further solidifying identity	No intact family from which to emancipate results in accelerated emancipation	One home base with specific evenings, weekends, and activities at the other home scheduled for regularity and predictability	One home base with 1 to 3 weekend visits per month at other home, depending on distance and capacity to travel	Possible acting out: drugs, sex, religion to attain a sense of belonging
Mourning the loss of childhood, dependency, protection within the family	Possible de-idealization of one or both parents	OR	Establish "permanent schedule" with some flexibility built in	Delayed entry into adolescence
Handling sexual feelings	Embarrassment about family	Equal basis with each parent is possible, up to two weeks in each residence	Adolescent input essential, adolescent cannot be forced into schedule he/she had no involvement in creating	Doubts about own relationship capacity: too much investment in relationships or withdrawal from relationships
Establishing sense of self vis-a-vis rules and regulations of society	Distress over parents' more obvious sexuality	OR	Non-residential parent will travel to home base to involve self with teachers, instructors, to attend performances and important events	
	Child will place peer needs ahead of family and therefore may not want to visit	"Nesting": both parents moving in and out of same residence is another possibility	Half of Christmas break, all of spring break with non-residential parent	
		Establish "permanent schedule" with some flexibility built in	If too far for regular weekends, then Thanksgiving and Presidents' Day weekend as well as entire summer spent with non-residential parent	
		Adolescent input essential, adolescent cannot be forced into schedule he/she had no involvement in creating		
		Maintain child's accessibility to school, peers, extracurricular and community involvements from both homes		

Chapter One:

"I'm Abandoned"
Infancy to Two and a Half Years

Developmental Tasks

INFANTS

Children begin, in the first year of life, a continuing process of learning both cognitively and emotionally about themselves and others. The foundation for many important issues is in the first year of life but these issues are not finished and left behind as the first year draws to a close. They set the pace, the tone, and the sense for many experiences that will follow and therein rests the reason for their extraordinary importance. Two of the most important issues that last a lifetime begin in infancy: attachment and trust.

Children form an attachment through a gradual process of having basic needs met by someone who, for example, attends when they cry, feeds and comforts when they are hungry or upset. Infants, totally unable to meet any of their own needs, are utterly dependent on a caretaker to provide this care for them. Infants begin to trust that needs will be met and that the world is a safe place in which to live through the gradual course of experience. They form attachments to a primary caretaking person who satisfies their needs and relieves their discomfort and fear. Through reliance on this initial attachment, infants develop trust and a sense of confidence which enables them to develop into individuals capable of enjoying human relationships.

At about two to three months of age, there is a notable increase in infants' interest in others and mutual play; smiling begins to take on social meaning (Emde, Gaensbauer, & Harmon, 1976). Through increased social interaction, infants gradually learn about the expression of their own feelings and the reactions of their primary caretakers. For example, babies smile and parents smile back; cries of hunger become different from cries for comforting. Communications become more purposeful and interactive. In summary, the comforting relationship and trust with the primary caretaker is being established.

Another notable increase in development takes place again at seven to nine months of age. Strangers elicit a fearful, distress reaction when they approach babies older than eight or nine months of age. Research (Emde et al., 1976) demonstrates that wariness and fear of unfamiliar situations is a prominent concern at this age. At seven to nine months, infants also react painfully to the loss of their primary caretaker. Spitz and Wolf (1946) first described this when they observed hospitalized infants who appeared withdrawn, apprehensive and sad. Many even stopped growing and developing; some died. All of the infants who reacted so intensely to the hospital experience were older than six months. Since this finding forty years ago, professionals caring for infants have recognized the serious consequences which separation from the primary caretaker can have.

It is not clear whether infants have the capacity to remember their primary caretaker when that person is out of their sight. From observational studies, we do know that when someone important in an infant's life disappears, even briefly, the infant appears anxious and fearful. When there is an actual extended loss of contact with the primary caretaker, these fearful reactions begin to predominate and can interfere with further development.

TODDLERS

During the second year of life, children, now toddlers, expand their awareness of themselves and the world through increased social relatedness and verbal communication. Toddlers are starting to feel more independent and less in need of the primary caretaker's constant presence. Comfort for children up to two and a half derives from having a strong sense of connection to the special somebody, the primary caretaker, who is meeting their basic needs and interacting with them in an attuned, predictable manner. As toddlers mature, they take pleasure in games that include running out of a room and peeking around a corner to make sure mother or father is still there. You will often see toddlers in stores with their parents, laughing in glee as they run away, but becoming quite horrified if they turn around and suddenly cannot find their parents. Child psychologists and psychiatrists call this activity "refueling" (Mahler, 1979; Kaplan, 1978). Children need to check back frequently with the primary source of nurturing to feel that source is still there for them and be reassured that basic needs will be met. They also check back for another important reason, which might be called "emotional reaffirmation." Now that toddlers have more self awareness and independence, they reaffirm that their primary caretaker is sharing in their subjective experience of the world by their checking back behavior. Stern (1985) explains that "an infant experiencing fear after wandering too far needs to know that his or her state of fear has been heard. It is more than a need to be held or soothed; it is also an inter-subjective need to be understood."

There is increased interest in and an increased capacity to explore the world that emerges in the second year of a child's life. Thinking skills have been evolving simultaneously with physical growth. By age two, children have the motor capacity to walk on their own and to feed themselves. Most two year olds can label and talk in two to three word sentences. It is generally not until children are around age three that they can communicate in full sentences. Although two year olds cannot verbally express much about their feelings, they are starting to develop the capacity to grasp symbolic ideas and to apply learning gained from one situation to another. The capacity to use symbols for comfort, rather than needing the actual presence of the primary caretaking person, is important because it means the child is gradually developing the ability to feel safe and comfortable in the world away from a primary caretaker.

Toddlers derive feelings of comfort from familiar toys and objects that are associated with pleasant moments spent in interaction with their primary caretakers. Children out shopping at the grocery store or a doctor's appointment often lug along a worn out toy because it allows them to venture into a new and unfamiliar situation while retaining a connection to the familiar environment of home and of the primary caretaker. The special blanket or toy symbolizes comfort and security because of its connection to the primary caretaker and familiar environment. Because such objects help children to make the transition from familiar environments to unfamiliar environments, they are called "transitional objects." Using a transitional object when in a new environment is one way for the toddler to feel assured that a primary caretaker and familiar environment still exist even when out of sight. The loss of the primary caretaker is the most deep seated fear the toddler has.

Residence and Visitation Recommendations

When determining residence and visitation in this developmental stage, a critical consideration is defining the nurturing individuals, environments, and objects. For an infant or toddler who is struggling to master the concept that someone out of sight can and will return, it is imperative that time away from the primary parent be brief.

To formulate a psychologically sound residence and visitation arrangement, it is necessary to assess who is the more psychologically comforting parent for a child. This is not a lofty concept by any means — quite the contrary. For a child up to age two and one half, the way to determine who is the more psychologically comforting parent is to quantitatively examine the history of caretaking. For example, who has changed what proportion of the child's diapers, who has handled what proportion of feedings, who has provided what proportion of comforting, hugging and caretaking while the infant has been sick. Appendix B provides a checklist to assist parents in making this determination.

In most instances, a primary caretaking parent can be determined. However, as parents increasingly share the responsibilities of child-rearing, a very young child may have been equally cared for by both parents. In this instance, it is not suggested that strong attachments be severed, but it is recommended that the very young child remain in one environment. Parents who have flexibility in their schedules, which they must both have had previously to qualify as primary caretakers, may be able to continue to share daytime caretaking while the young child returns to always sleep in the same place.

If as parents you cannot agree on the answers to the questions defining the primary caretaker, you will need to bring in an expert to decide your child's residence. However, if you are able to agree on the answers to these questions, it is recommended that for a child up to age two and one half the primary home be with the more frequent caretaker.

During this early period of children's lives, it is important for the non-residential or visiting parent to step aside somewhat — albeit only temporarily. There is no need at this developmental level to rush building the attachment to a parent who has been less active prior to this time. Opportunity for attachment will come later. If there is disruption in allowing a child to build a secure sense of trust and attachment to the primary caretaking parent, there may be interference with that child's capacity to form relationships later in life. Because very little is known about the effects of dual primary parenting on the very young child, it is recommended that the conservative approach be taken, that of opting for what is known about healthy emotional development.

If the caretaking relationship has not already been established on a fairly equal basis, then equalizing the parenting is to be initiated gradually rather than suddenly. A workable visitation recommendation is for children to have short, frequent contacts with the non-residential or visiting parent.

In summary, it is suggested that infants up to about age two and one half reside with the person who has done the primary caretaking. The other parent should have short visits lasting between an hour or two, on a daily basis if possible. As children adjust to the parental separation, the amount of visitation time can be increased very gradually.

Initially, overnights are not recommended. Nighttime is often an uncomfortable period for young children. When they are tired, the defenses they have to cope with stress and anxiety are depleted. Night is not a time when children are going to be building an attachment or relating; it is a time when they are going to be sleeping, hopefully. Sleeping away from their primary home, in an environment separate from their primary caretaking parent, can be frightening for infants and young children. To insist on overnight visitation during this stage may be more of a deterrent than a progressive step toward the goal of strengthening the relationship between an infant and the non-residential parent.

Again, a major task of this developmental stage is to build the foundations for later relationships. While it is essential to maintain and enlarge the relationship between the infant and non-residential parent, it should be done gradually. Comfortable familiarity with the non-residential parent's environment must be established before there can be overnights.

Occasionally, one parent moves a great distance from the other. When the child is in infancy, it is recommended that one of the parents travel in either direction to enable both parents to spend time with the child. Infants to age two and a half are not capable of traveling alone on any form of transportation in order to visit. Either the non-residential parent should go to where the infant resides as frequently as possible and/or the residential parent may travel with the infant to the vicinity of the distant parent. Out-of-state visits, lengthy overnights, and vacations with the non-residential parent are strongly urged **against** during this early period. However, it is important that the non-residential parent maintains a continuing relationship with the child throughout this developmental stage. Suggestions for maintaining long distance relationships between visits are contained in Appendix C.

The goal of visitation for this developmental stage is best viewed as building increasing familiarity between the non-residential parent and the child. The non-residential parent may need to be reassured that growth toward his or her role as an equal co-parent is supported by the residential parent and that the sought after equality will evolve a bit further down the road. By the end of this stage, once weekly overnights may be introduced if the non-residential parent has been actively participating in caretaking. But again, this kind of visitation should begin only after a comforting role for the non-residential parent has been established. Another circumstance in which the possibility of an overnight visit may be considered is when there is an older sibling of at least age five years, who has an established relationship with the non-residential parent and who will be accompanying the toddler-aged child on a visit. An older sibling can be of tremendous transitional comfort to a younger child.

Risks

If separation from the primary caretaker takes place abruptly, there is a risk that a young child will exhibit symptoms of stress. It is important that parents be able to detect this phenomenon when it occurs.

Young children may experience a tremendous amount of dismay or disorientation upon realizing that they have lost contact with their primary caretaking parent. Anxiety symptoms will appear and be expressed differently in each child. These may include crying, irritability, disorientation, and possibly tantrums. The most pervasive symptom is regression, i.e., immature behavior or losing control of previously mastered skills and functions. If children's anxiety goes unaddressed, they may begin to show signs of panic when confronting separation from the primary caretaking parent. Additionally, there may be a loss of the capacity to develop good relationships and many superficial attachments may be formed by these children instead. Such children may appear to be extremely needy of physical affection and may seek it indiscriminately. As children grow older, another manifestation of anxiety might be the hoarding of food or objects which the children use to comfort themselves. These behaviors may symbolize feelings about being deprived of the primary relationship in their lives from which they derive comfort.

While some transitional stress is predictable when changing caretakers, it is recommended that parents watch for these behaviors and discontinue overnights or shorten the length of daytime visits for a while if symptoms appear and persist. The short-term risk in making residence and visitation arrangements that go beyond a child's developmental maturity is that the child will manifest symptoms of anxiety. If parents recognize a consistent pattern of symptoms emerging, it is recommended that they temporarily back up and adopt a set of residence and visitation arrangements applicable to an earlier stage of development.

The longer-term risk is that a child will not have formed a solid primary attachment foundation. Without such a sense of attachment, children do not develop a healthy sense of themselves as individuals; they do not progress to later developmental stages comfortably. There is often difficulty mastering learning tasks, forming friendships, going off to school; in summary, performing tasks that require spending more time without the primary caretaker. Such children may carry unresolved issues from this stage into later stages of development. How large a toll is taken on these children's personalities depends on how significant and frequent past losses have been and on how resilient they are as individuals.

Special Circumstances

Making sensible residential and visitation decisions means putting animosity aside in serving the best interests of the children. Sometimes mothers, who have been the primary caretakers while dads work, tend to doubt seriously the father's parenting capacity. These mothers feel that their doubts represent reasonable grounds for withholding the child from the father. It is essential to understand, however, that fathers play an important socializing role in the development of children. In infancy, children will benefit by establishing a familiarity and a comfort in being parented by their fathers as well as by their mothers.

Recently, a phone call was received from a judge who had ordered a mother and father to seek psychological counseling so that they would change the residence and visitation schedule as their eight month old infant matured and his psychological needs changed. In this instance, the infant was going to reside initially with the mother but have frequent visits with the father. The mother expressed tremendous concern that the father probably would not feed the baby his vegetables while the baby was visiting in the middle of the day. In this situation, the mother experienced her parenting role as so exclusively her domain that she could not acknowledge that the father could adequately handle the job; she failed to understand that he had something valuable to contribute.

While a father may not feed the baby the bottle or the vegetables in quite the same way as mother, a father has many unique and important functions to perform in an infant's life. A father's interactions with his children have a great deal to do with the children being able to form healthy self concepts as females or males later in life and also with their ability to form relationships with peers. According to Brazelton (Brazelton, 1984),

> *For a baby, having an active, involved father is not the same as simply having more mothering... Where there is an active father, the child grows up to be more successful at school, to have a better sense of humor and to get along better with other kids. He believes more in himself and is better motivated to learn.*

Some parents withhold visitation because they have a need to express power in the context of the former marital relationship. This is especially true in marital relationships where there has been violence or intimidation of one by the other. Again, if these issues cannot be resolved by the mutual agreement of both parties, then an expert must be brought in to help evaluate the situation and recommend remedies.

In using these guidelines, parents must maintain flexibility in revising the residence and visitation schedule so that the child's psychological needs are being met appropriately. As the child grows into later developmental stages, it is recommended that parents refer to later chapters of this book and adjust accordingly the residence and visitation arrangements.

Chapter Two:

"I'm Responsible"
Two and a Half to Five Years

During the preschool years, children continue their growth as individuals separate from their parents. They are now able to evoke and hold in mind a mental image of the comforting parent when separated from him or her for lengthy periods of time. That is, children no longer rely solely on the familiar environment or their parent's actual physical presence for comfort. The negativism and power struggling evident in children of this age is due to their growing sense of emerging individualism. Children who feel secure are now beginning to test parental limits. This testing involves progressing with a given activity until a "no" is heard. One crucial function of testing limits is for children to discover the consequences of overstepping limits. They wonder if they still will be loved if they oppose a parent's will. The primary fear of the preschool aged children is of losing parental approval and parental love.

Children of this age are also beginning to struggle within themselves over conflicting feelings (i.e., growing up vs. staying little, loving someone vs. hating someone, being a boy vs. being a girl, being powerful vs. being helpless). Because power versus helplessness is a central issue for children at this age, they frequently incorporate powerful superheroes in their play. They enjoy using Superman, Wonder Woman, and other characters in order to play out themes of power and control. Simultaneously, they are engaged in real life battles around eating, toilet behavior, bathing, hygiene, and other areas involving control over bodily functions. These confrontations represent one way in which children express their sense of individuality. In the battlefield for control of bodily functions, the children soon learn that they will be victorious in gaining control of their own bodies: "I can eat what I want, when I want, and you can't make me." In these struggles, parents may first recognize their own powerlessness. While well-intentioned parents may coax, encourage, and state values, ultimately it is the children's judgment that must come into play in deciding how and when to exercise bodily functions.

Critical throughout the second year and into the third are major language milestones. With the onset of language development comes mastery of key concepts particularly relevant to our discussion of visitation arrangements. For the first time children can understand the essence of time-oriented ideas such as "We will be returning to mother tomorrow." Repetition of such phrases enables children to sustain themselves through many difficulties that may arise from separation. Along with comprehension, children are simultaneously becoming more capable in the use of expressive language as well. For the first time, they can give verbal feedback about the success of visits or the difficulties experienced with separation. For the first time parents can ascertain from children facts and feelings about what did and what did not go well during visits.

There is a need for direct and frequent explanations and comforting from parents since children of divorce may continue to experience a great deal of anxiety about being abandoned. This anxiety is not as disorganizing as it was at the previous stage. For example, children use the medium of play to act out their anxieties and fears toward gaining a sense of mastery over them. They use play to express positive emotions as well. Dollhouses, puppet play, and drawing are frequently easier channels for self-expression than the use of direct statements. Child therapists often use these media to help children express feelings. Those parents who introduce these activities themselves report satisfaction and joy in participating with their children as well.

As they progress through this stage, children develop increasing capacity to accept the limits that are placed on them. They are developing a more complex sense of identity, working on internalizing controls, and they are building a moral and ethical code, a conscience, by internalizing the voices and the images of their parents.

Toward the end of this stage, at about four to five years of age, children enter a phase traditionally labeled "the Oedipal stage" of development. At this point, children refocus their power struggle from the relatively pristine willfulness around control of bodily functions and independence to a more interpersonal orientation. They now attempt to step into the arena of the parental sexual relationship. Don't panic! This merely translates behaviorally into an emerging awareness of the parental sex differences and frequently a longing to spend more time with the opposite-sex parent.

Witness the five year old boy baking cookies with mom, stating to her, "Mommy, I enjoy being with you so much, I'd like to marry you and bake cookies every day." The resolution of this issue may be easier for the married parents, who only need to point to their marital status as a statement of their unavailability. Imagine the four year old girl reading on her divorced daddy's lap, who expresses her wish to be with daddy "happily ever after." The growth-fostering dad's reaction may be "Someday you will probably want to choose your very own person. But I can see that right now you like our special time together."

Characteristic of the entire preschool stage is the emergence of the concept of "magical thinking." Children of four or five years of age feel that what they do or think has an effect on their environment, whether a causal relationship can or cannot be demonstrated. Following the story line of the Greek tragedy Oedipus Rex, children of four or five years of age fantasize the achievement of some sort of special union or coalition with the opposite-sex parent, and simultaneously wish to do away with the same-sex parent.

Whether parents are together or apart, a satisfactory resolution of this phase occurs when both parents remain patient and involved. Ultimately, the child resolves this developmental dilemma through identification, i.e., an attempt to emulate or "be just like," the same-sex parent. Increased interest in peers, school, and activities also helps by refocusing the child on issues outside the immediate family environment. Power-oriented interactions finally yield to a sense of more cooperative relating, coinciding with the child's transition into school.

Divorce Issues

Psychologist Judith Wallerstein (1983) points out that for preschoolers of divorced parents, the logistics of visiting are critical. Her staff devised a board version of a visiting game where parents or therapists take a child back and forth in imagination from mom's house to dad's house, encountering various obstacles along the way. Allowing children to regulate and address the perceived hazards of visitation imparts a sense of mastery over their anxieties. It also provides a forum for the expression of any additional visiting concerns they may have experienced. Wallerstein and Kelly (1975) have noted that, because children at this stage are so acutely aware of their dependence on parents, children involved with divorce demonstrate a great deal of despair and much concern about having their basic needs met. Concurrently, parents in the throes of separation often have some diminished parenting capacity due to other stresses they are under at this time. As children perceive this, they begin to experience a fear of losing both of their parents and manifest anxiety about who is going to meet their basic needs. Children from two and a half to five years of age can imagine the future and can become tremendously fearful that if one of their parents has left, the other parent may abandon them too, leaving no one to take care of them.

Regression is a characteristic stress reaction seen in children of this age whose parents are divorcing. That is, they adopt behaviors characteristic of earlier developmental levels. Parents may find that bedwetting begins to recur. Perhaps children will have to return to the comfort of previously used transitional objects such as a favorite blanket or special toy. There may be a loss of toilet training formerly attained, or the emergence of sleeping and eating disturbances, or thumb sucking. A brief period of regression is predictable for children of this age.

As uncertainties diminish in the new environment, readjustment to the new circumstances should include a regaining of previously mastered functions within three to six months. If the regressed condition persists beyond such a reasonable readjustment period, parents might well consider the services of a mental health professional for their child.

It is important for parents to understand that it is normal for children during this stage to manifest sadness and depression for brief periods of time. Typically their sad periods are interspersed with a return to their normal level of activity and involvement with outside activities.

Understanding the Oedipal wish and the use of magical thinking, parents may then imagine how it is possible for the child of four or five years of age, whose same-sex parent moves out of the household, to be left feeling horrifyingly powerful. Children fantasize the notion that they have been responsible on some level for the separation of their parents, that it was probably their behavior, something that they did or did not do, that caused their separation. Repeated reassurance that they are not the cause of the change in the parents' relationship, as well as the parents' understanding of this persistent fantasy, are required to help address the children's feelings of responsibility. Conversely, children who view themselves as powerful enough to have caused the parental separation in the first place feel they must then be powerful enough to reverse the effect they have had. At this developmental stage, if you ask children whose parents have divorced, "What are you doing to try to bring your parents back together?" most will have a ready reply available. Alyssa, age four, had a fantasy of reuniting her parents by inviting them both to a tea party where they would fall in love with each other again. Josh, age five, initially appearing to be free of symptoms, reported that he was on his best behavior because he believed it was his bad behavior that had caused the breakup of his parents in the first place. Finally, Amy, a kindergarten-age child, repeatedly acted out in an attempt to reunite her parents who would both show up at the school principal's office when called. In order to counteract the persistent notion by children that they are responsible for the parents' divorce and have the power to reverse the separation, it is important that parents frequently reassure their children that they are not at fault and are not responsible for the separation and divorce.

Both parents continue to be of prime importance to children. Because of the dominance of the children's internal power struggle, this is an easy age for children to play one parent against the other. It is important for parents who share in the parenting of children after divorce to be cautious of the fact that these children now have language which will enable them to carry stories back and forth. This can facilitate the pitting of one parent against the other. It is most important that the parents communicate with each other, that they be flexible, and that they not believe **everything** they are told by their children!

Residence and Visitation Recommendations

For two and a half to five year olds, parents may divide the responsibilities of parenting and overnight stays proportionately to the amount of time each has spent meeting the child's needs prior to this point. A few children in this age range are able to handle a half-time living arrangement with each parent in a comfortable way. This, however, is the exception. Parenting prior to divorce has rarely been divided fifty-fifty for children age two and a half to five. In most instances, mom has been the primary parent for the young child. Whatever the prior circumstances, it is advisable to minimize the length of any one visit away from their primary residence, still opting for shorter, more frequent visits. For example, it is less stressful for a child to spend one or two overnights and then return to the residential parent's house for a few days before the next overnight, rather then to spend as much as half a week to a week at one house and then the other. Keep in mind that children of two and a half and three years of age are still mastering the developmental tasks associated with independence. They may experience acute feelings of loss and separation from one or both parents during intervals of absence for as long as a week. Sustaining a feeling of attachment is still critical.

Another important factor for children of two and a half to five years of age is that they need each parent's sanction of their relationship with the other parent. While it may be difficult for some parents with lingering animosities toward their ex-spouses, parents must demonstrate support and sanction the children's maximizing their attachment to the opposite parent. This may be achieved by allowing and assisting them in telephone calling, as well as by tolerating and enjoying stories they may present of what they are doing with the other parent.

Children of this age can give verbal feedback as to how well they are functioning both in their primary residence and on visits. By the age of three, children are typically able to articulate their feelings, to verbalize their fears, and to give parents direct feedback about the workability of a particular residence and visitation arrangement. Parents are advised to seek such feedback in regular conversations without "prying," and to return to earlier patterns of visitation if their children are reporting stress or exhibiting regressed behaviors.

The aim of these residence and visitation arrangements is to build relationships that will last a lifetime between the parents and the child. Moving too quickly into lengthy visits could have an opposite, potentially disruptive, effect on the relationship-building process. It is advisable that parents adopt an earlier set of recommendations for a regressed or fearful child, and stay with that schedule for several months until the child is reassured and functioning at an appropriate developmental level.

Jordon, age five, had been placed in an ill-advised arrangement for his developmental stage allowing for one week with each parent. He had begun to exhibit aggressive behaviors when he was with his mother. In contrast, when he was with his father, he seemed to be very sad. When at his father's house, Jordon was intensely longing for his mother. He would draw pictures for her, listen to her favorite music, and frequently request to call her. How ironic that when he was with the mother, for whom he longed, Jordon manifested extremely angry and intolerant behavior. The boy was angry at his mother for what he perceived as her abandonment of him. His symptomatic behavior lessened when the visitation schedule was adjusted to two overnights a week with dad and the rest of the week with mom.

An effective arrangement when the second-home parent works a typical five-day business week is the "long weekend-short weekend" visitation schedule. In this arrangement, the second-home parent would have the child for one overnight every other weekend and two overnights on the alternate weekends. This arrangement might be interspersed with at least one weekday visit. It is important that the second-home parent build parenting skill and comfort in child care and that both parent and child grow comfortably close over a period of time.

In many instances, parents do not wish to establish fifty-fifty split time. Such an arrangement frequently is not suitable due to work schedules or other adult needs. Parents, dads as well as moms, should inventory their own needs and desires as to how much time they wish to be available for active parenting. It is important that time spent with the child is spent actively parenting whenever possible. Quality time with the child will be experienced if visits do not feel obligatory or intrusive. Remember that parenting often involves putting adult needs second. Parents must always be honest with themselves in considering how much time they wish to share with the child.

To determine which household should be made the child's primary residence, it is necessary to determine who is the primary source of nurturing for the child. Again, the child's primary attachment can be determined best by history (see Appendix B). Parents need to be cautioned against asking their children direct questions about their preferences. Children often will respond with what they think the questioning parent wants to hear. When they know parents are separating, children will try not to lose an alliance with either parent. They are more likely to respond to a neutral figure, such as an evaluator or a therapist, with more accurate answers to direct questions about their preferences.

Projective techniques may help professionals assess children of this age. Children express themselves through drawings, stories, and by verbalizing their fantasies. A therapist can help parents to understand and interpret the child's feelings about supportiveness and attachment. If parents come to a fundamental impasse and cannot determine which household should be the primary residence, they should consult a mental health professional.

Many parents like to travel longer distances for longer periods of time during vacation periods. Often this involves visits to extended family or the parent's childhood home. Vacation periods for children in this two and a half to five year old age group should be limited to several two to six day blocks of time spent away from either parent throughout the year. Keep in mind that laying aside major vacation adventures is a temporary phenomenon and goes along with the turf of having young children. Children of two and a half to five years do not get much out of a grand tour of Europe or even of a neighboring state. They would prefer to interact with their parents, participating in activities which are age-appropriate for them, even if that means just helping around the house. For example, Sandra, age four, who resides primarily with her mom, was about to start a week-long visit with her dad in another part of the country. She clearly feared that she would have difficulty maintaining a mental image of her mother to whom she evidenced primary attachment. She projected this fear onto the mother, however, by expressing a strong concern that mom would not remember her or that mom would forget that she was Sandra's parent. This fear was dissipated by mom's arranging to send a post card midway through the visit. Sandra also carried mom's photograph with her and knew that mom would be carrying her photograph as well. In addition, time was prearranged for the mother to be available on the telephone. All this was successful in helping Sandra to keep the mental image of mom in mind and the visit with dad was a success.

If parents have moved a great distance from each other, it is advisable that one of the parents travel to the residential area of the other. Establish a visitation pattern consisting of two to three day maximum stays with the second-home parent. When the second home parent travels to the geographical area of the primary parent, this may mean the two to three day visit will take place at a local hotel, motel or home of a mutual friend. Between visits a return to the primary home parent is essential to include time for the child's feelings of attachment, support, and acceptance to be replenished.

To summarize the logical visitation and custody recommendations for two and a half to five year olds: parents might try sharing parenting in the proportion to which they have shared parenting in the past. For instance, if the father or mother cared for the child approximately 20 percent of the pre-divorce time, then 20 percent of that child's week should be spent with that parent post-divorce. The time spent on visits can be increased as the relationship with the formerly less involved parent builds and is strengthened. Overnight stays at the second home certainly begin to make sense for the two and a half to five year old. If the child does well with this initial arrangement, visitation gradually can be increased. Solo out-of-state visitation is not recommended in this stage.

Risks

Parents note that children often have trouble making the transition from one parent's home to the other's. It is not unusual, for example, for a child to return from a visit with mother or father tearful, upset and a little bit regressed. Things may not be going wrong at the other household. Rather, the child may be having difficulty in shifting gears, finding it hard to leave one parent and return to the other.

Children evidence some actual mourning for the absent parent during transitions, especially during an initial adjustment to a visitation schedule. Parents need to note if these anxiety feelings persist for more than a half day to a day during the process of reentering a parent's home. Listen for the child's expressed concerns regarding visits. If a pattern of anxiety and regression is persistent and regular, the possibility exists that visits with the non-residential parent are too long or that they are too stressful for the child. It may be necessary to use the visitation recommendations for an earlier developmental stage. Conversely, if things are going very well and the child is showing little difficulty during transitions from one parent to the other, then visitation can gradually be increased to longer periods of time.

Children may be helped immensely during transitions by prior planning of a special reentry activity. For example, looking forward to the preparation of a special dinner, playing a designated game, or entertaining a special friend or relative upon returning home often helps ease the sense of loneliness that may accompany transitions.

Children experience markedly more difficulty when parents utilize face-to-face contact during transition time in order to express unresolved anger to each other or when they use this opportunity to bicker or argue about the visitation schedule. If parents cannot disengage from expressing anger toward each other at these times, it is advisedly better to send the child out alone from the front door to the car door, thereby avoiding any face-to-face contact.

Children who are unable to master the developmental tasks for two and a half to five years go through subsequent ages with low self esteem, conflict with parents and continuing power struggles more appropriate to this earlier stage. They delay settling the psychological conflicts whose resolution would lead to more cooperative relationships. Instead, they often feel compelled to stubbornly challenge limits, and are quite negative or aggressive. Their defiance and negativism may cause problems with both teachers and peers. These behaviors handicap such children in successfully negotiating friendships in the school environment.

As noted earlier, children who are experiencing excessive stress are at risk to regress or adopt other behaviors characteristic of an earlier age. Regression may cause even further interference with their continuing development. For example, children who wet the bed may be fearful of going on overnights to other children's homes, something that youngsters like to do at ages six, seven, or eight.

The secure child is ready by five or six to start moving away from the home environment, to start concentrating energy more toward mastery of learning, friendships, peer groups, games, sports, hobbies, and other activities away from the home. The child who has not mastered the tasks of the earlier stage still must cope with school and the pressures it may bring. Most children begin going to school by age five, whether or not they are considered emotionally ready. Remaining regressed and immature when beginning school ultimately takes a serious toll on the child's self-concept due to experiences of rejection by other children and teachers who do not find them to be rewarding individuals. These children may grow to dislike themselves as well.

Additional risks include the feeling of responsibility for the divorce due to the magical thinking, discussed earlier. These children may persist in attempting to reunite their parents by displaying either positive or negative behaviors unless their fantasies of responsibility are addressed and put aside. In these instances, statements about the child's lack of responsibility must be repeated frequently.

Special Circumstances

Children between three and five may be able to tolerate lengthier out-of-state visits if they have established dual geographic familiarity. An illustration is a case where a mom with primary residence moved out of state with her four year old. The boy was able to return easily to his former home for week-long stays with his dad. Although the father had been less of an involved caretaker, he lived in familiar surroundings with a great deal of extended family. In addition, he continued to maintain contact with the mom's extended family. In this instance, the parents agreed that each would provide transportation in one direction.

When more than one child is involved, parents should arrange at least occasional one-to-one interaction with each child, rather than always moving a "set of siblings" together. When one-to-one visits are instituted with a child formerly always seen as one of a group of two or more, both the parent and the child are likely to discover new things about each other. Getting out of the sibling role, such as "the baby," "the bully," or "the scapegoat" can be rewarding and self-esteem enhancing for the child.

For example, Mark, age four, and Megan, age seven, always had joint visits with their father. The visits were not working out successfully. A recommendation was made that the father arrange for Megan to visit on a schedule appropriate for her level of development, while Mark would visit on a schedule appropriate for his level of development. The schedule was such that Megan and Mark each had one-to-one visitation times as well as periodically overlapping visitation times. Dad was able to enjoy his children individually and together. All family members subsequently reported more satisfactory visits.

Many parents voice concerns regarding the effects of separating siblings from each other. As a general rule, the parent-child inter-action needs to take precedence for each sibling. Where there is shared parenting, as there was in the above instance, children actually benefit from periodic separations from their siblings. In most instances, the relationship with each parent is enhanced and strengthened by at least occasional one-to-one experiences.

In making a decision to create separate primary residences for siblings, the guiding principle, as always, is to minimize losses for the child. While siblings should have experiences living together in each household whenever possible, it is the parent-child relationship that is more critical with respect to maximizing the child's psychological development.

In another instance, divorced parents of two girls and a boy were bogged down with visitation and vacation plan disagreements. The parents had set a precedent of "fairness" with their children, which meant that if one child went somewhere, the other children had to go. The parents had inadvertently empowered their children with tremendous manipulative tools. When the children sang the tune, "It's not fair," these parents would go to great tension-filled lengths attempting to rectify the situation. Some weeks after strug-gling with the introduction of the new concept that "life is not always fair," the parents were able to tailor their visitation sched-ules so that their teenage son's visitation schedule allowed for more time with his dad; their daughter in her later elementary years had her visitation schedule adjusted to allow more time with her mother; and the younger sister, a five year old, reported delight and satis-faction in living with mom and frequently visiting with dad.

Finally, parents must keep in mind that children should not be expected to adjust to living in a household where there is fear. Children should not live with a parent who is violent. Neither should children live with a parent who is alcoholic or involved with drugs to the point that he or she does not exercise good judgment; nor should children live with a parent who is emotionally disturbed to the point where he or she does not adequately supervise or care for the children. Once again, the guidelines set forth in this book cannot be applied to family circumstances such as these.

If you do have concerns, it would be best to contact an evaluator or mental health counselor for advice in making decisions about visitation. If a parent's home is determined not to be a safe envi-ronment for a child, the professionals might recommend, for example, that the child be able to visit with that parent in an office of someone who will be able to supervise the visit. In this way, the child will have an opportunity to spend some time with that parent. At a point when that parent is, if ever, sufficiently rehabilitated as judged by a trained professional or otherwise becomes equipped to handle a more normalized visitation situation, new arrangements can be made.

Chapter Three:

"I'm Not Fitting In"
Six to Eight Years Old

Developmental Tasks

The hallmark emotional task of six to eight year olds is their active participation in a process of branching out from the family. This is the stage during which children begin the transition away from home into relationships with friends, hobbies, activities, and the school environment. Children have a favorite teacher at school and, frequently, a number of friends often labeled as "my very best friend" or "my number two or my number three friend." Suddenly, children of this age do not want to spend as much time at home. Parents report feeling like a chauffeur, escorting children from one activity to another.

All of this occurs because of the enormous intellectual and emotional growth that has taken place during the preschool years. By the age of six children have far more capacity for separation; they can tolerate longer and longer periods of time away from home without mounting anxiety and fear. They are past the age of thinking and feeling that their parents may not exist when they are out of sight. Emotional development has progressed to the point that children of this age can maintain a sense of internal security and self-soothing. Methods of mastering anxiety and inhibiting impulses have been learned during the first six years of life and the primary developmental tasks extend beyond the family domain. Six to eight year old children are building a sense of mastery and a sense of self-esteem by relating to others through friendships and activities. This is a crucial age for sex role identification and for the building of confidence and self-esteem.

Children who have developed successfully up to this point have fairly organized moods and emotions. Now feelings are generally shared directly and verbally; fantasy play diminishes. At this age you can talk directly to children in order to learn how they feel, relying less on learning from their behavioral cues. Fine motor skills have developed to the point where children, who are less verbal, can share their feelings through creative arts, typically without the concerns about critical appraisal by others that emerge later.

One of the primary tools psychologists use in assessing children of this age is to request that they draw a picture of their family. This task poses a dilemma for children of divorce because they must decide who to include in their drawing and how to place them on the page. A picture that appeared on a magazine cover some years ago illustrated this dilemma well. The child drew an elaborate house which was clearly divided down the middle. Placed in the middle wall was a tiny door which only a child could fit through. One side contained father and the other mother. While the door was large enough to allow the child to visit both parents, they could not fit through the door. Therefore, they could not fight. This picture communicated directly what children of this age need—namely to be in contact with both of their parents, in a safe environment without conflict and fighting.

Self-concept development is crucial at this age, including the continuing development of gender identity. Children need to interact with both mother and father to experience how they are responded to by an adult female and male. Out of this interaction will emerge a sense of what is valued about their maleness or femaleness; this conscious and unconscious sensitivity forms the basis for the child's moving into intimate relationships which will occur during adolescence and beyond.

Parents also impart to their children a sense of values and social ideals. At approximately age six, guilt for wrong-doing begins to develop, a sense of empathy first starts, and social behavior norms begin to become incorporated into what will be the adult personality.

The most pervasive feeling experienced by children of six to eight whose parents are divorcing is sadness and despair. The capacity for greater emotional expression at this age means that more internal sadness will be displayed when a loss occurs. Children in this stage are less likely to use fantasy to deny unpleasant aspects of the real world. Because they can no longer fool themselves into believing that the unpleasantness is not truly happening, they may suffer enormous and sometimes overwhelming grief. Kelly and Wallerstein (1976) discuss the sense of deprivation that these children feel. Children from six to eight worry if there will be enough to eat, enough money for other necessities, a place to live, and most serious of all, if their parents will leave them too, as they left each other. Some worry that the divorce may mean they will have no family at all. The pain is obvious and very pervasive; these children look and act sad. Memories of the absent parent are often with them throughout the day; reminders are everywhere and concentration is very difficult. Attention in school is often affected. It is a common finding that there is interference with academic performance for a year's time or more (Guidubaldi, Cleminshaw, Perry, & McLoughlin, 1983). Teachers report that immediately after a separation or divorce children spend time in school just staring off into space. This is because they cannot concentrate; all they can think about is that their family is falling apart. In turn, their school work is affected and they begin to bring home lower or even failing grades. They may not want to participate in the fun sports and activities that they previously had enjoyed. They do not want to go to Brownies or to soccer practice. As the depression becomes more serious, some children will begin to isolate themselves. Because children from six to eight derive so much of their sense of worth from peers and school performance, a critical developmental task, that of developing self-worth, can be disturbed.

For children of six to eight a divorce is all too real and painful. These children have a sufficient awareness of the larger outside world to know what divorce means, and probably know other children who have been in this situation as well. Children of this age commonly resort to trickery, illness or accidents in an effort to bring their parents together again. The scheme individual children use is often dictated by what they have seen work in the past. Becoming hurt or sick is one of the most effective tools in all families to unite parents through worry and tragedy.

For example, Kate, a girl of seven, whose parents were divorced, thought that if she ate many, many bananas she surely would be sent to the hospital. Then both of her parents would have to come and take care of her. Thus, she ate an extraordinary number of bananas and, indeed, got sick. Of course, this did not bring her family back together again.

Some children take even more drastic measures than Kate. Their behavior can become quite frightening. Careless risk taking can be motivated by both sadness and the wish to reunite parents. Some children ride their bikes in unsafe places or ways, initiate play with objects like matches or firecrackers, or begin to express unusual physical complaints. Such behaviors not only put the child at risk for immediate physical harm, but also may lay the groundwork for later physical illnesses of psychological origin.

Children whose parents divorce at this stage experience multiple losses. While younger children lose a parent and often their primary home environment, children at this stage lose more. The sadness they feel from the loss of a parent at home, as well as from the loss of friends in the neighborhood and at school, teachers, activities and interests associated with their school and neighborhood environment, can no longer be pretended away. It is real and it hurts. They know what divorce means; it means the previous family situation is lost forever.

Residence and Visitation Recommendations

Again, minimizing loss is a critical principle to abide by for six to eight year old children. If at all possible, the best arrangement is for the second home parent to live either in close proximity to the children or transport them to the school that they have been attending, arrange visits with friends they have made, and maintain the out-of-school activities with which they have been involved. Children of six to eight can handle moving back and forth fairly freely between two different homes. Certainly, if there has been shared parenting up to this age, there can be a continuation of coparenting. Working out visitation arrangements in a way that minimizes losses for children is a critical dimension.

It is still simplest and psychologically wisest for most children from six to eight to have one home in which they live primarily. Children usually can tolerate a living arrangement which is almost fifty-fifty, possibly more like sixty-forty, as long as both parents are residing in reasonably close proximity and are willing to make themselves sufficiently flexible in transporting the child to away-from-home activities and peers who are important. Many children of six to eight can successfully live in one home for two or three weekdays and in the other for the remaining weekdays, while alternating weekends. Such an arrangement means, however, that each parent must provide transportation to school on some mornings and be willing to provide contact with friends and activities over the weekend.

A two-home arrangement, or *Mom's House-Dad's House* situation (Ricci, 1980), is possible for many children from six to eight. Most important, parents must be able to understand their children's needs. Some children who have established a primary residence are not yet ready for extended time away from that residence and they become disrupted by the back and forth arrangement. Overnights of one to three nights in succession are generally okay for most children of this age provided that they have established a relationship with the parent with whom they will be overnighting. If overnights are not working out, recommendations for preschool aged children should be followed until the closeness and comfort develops that will enable children to move, without undue stress, to recommendations for their current chronological age.

Half weeks, or half weeks with alternating weekends, is the preferable fifty-fifty arrangement for the six to eight year old child. In some instances, particularly as children get to the older end of this age group, they are able to handle a week with one parent and a week with the other parent. Such a fifty-fifty arrangement can only exist under circumstances where both parents have been participating fairly equally in the caretaking of the children and when they live in close proximity.

Six to eight years is the age at which children can tolerate out-of-state visitation. If one parent has moved out of state, the child can visit that parent in his or her home. It is essential that the visits be of relatively short duration, preferably no more than two weeks, with ample opportunity for maintaining contact as needed with the residential parent through phone calls and letters. Since frequent long distance visits are expensive for many families, Appendix C suggests the means to maintain a close emotional relationship at a distance.

At this age, an entire summer is too long a period to spend away from the residential parent. For some children, a maximum one month stay away from home is possible, especially if the child is visiting an area in which the child previously resided and where there has been fairly equal attachment formed to both parents. Again, arrangements should be made in relationship to the amount of activity and caretaking that has preceded this period. Nevertheless, a one month visit ought to be punctuated by reasonably frequent phone calls to the residential parent.

If possible, it is preferable that children have a number of different visits throughout the year and the summer, rather than one lengthy visit. For instance, a child could make three two-week visits away, which might be twice during a summer and possibly a Christmas vacation or a spring break. While on visits, children of six to eight years of age are still going to need help in communicating with the residential parent. In addition, they definitely need positive sanctioning from both parents to manage this successfully. There is a high degree of homesickness risk for children who have not been away previously, particularly where there has been unequal caretaking of a child. The non-residential parent needs to be sensitive to this possibility.

A parent dealing with a homesick child is advised to first listen to the child to determine what or who is being missed. The next step is to establish some feeling of linkage to the people or things being missed. Activities that help bridge one environment to another include phone calls, letter writing or special projects such as buying and sending a gift or taking photographs to share. Finally, a child is often comforted by reassurances that help to build a visual image of the people and place being missed. Describe what the other parent or siblings might be doing, assure the child that the house and belongings are still there, and talk sentimentally and kindly about the homesick feelings. Most children will readily verbalize their homesickness but parents are advised to watch for symptoms of depression and regression. If the homesick feelings persist, in spite of these efforts, the visit may have to be curtailed.

Parents try to seek creative solutions when their homes are located some distance from each other. Often times parents ask about the advisability of having the child live one school year with one parent and one school year with the other parent, attending different schools in different areas of the country. In our experience, this has been disruptive and unsatisfactory for children. Such a lifestyle is not conducive to a child's mastering a primary psychological task of this age, which is in part to develop feelings of investment in a neighborhood, community and peer relationships.

Risks

The primary risk for six to eight year old children is that so much confusion and disruption will be created by the parental separation that they fail to have an opportunity to form stable peer group relationships or enter into community activities. Children who attend one school while visiting one parent and another school while with the other parent lack the opportunity to enter into activities from which they will receive peer and adult feedback needed to develop a sense of self-worth. Finally, they may not have the sense of a secure home environment with a solid base from which to move away and begin to explore relationships with others that will prepare them for the tasks of later development. Such children are likely to feel confused. Children are extraordinarily sensitive to being left out, to not belonging, to feeling that they are not valued by their peers. Often, they conclude that something is wrong with them.

Academic difficulty is also a high risk factor for children whose parents divorce during this stage. Children of divorce have a high rate of poor school performance even when the divorce occurred under the most optimal conditions. Children from single parent homes are more likely to repeat a grade and are an average of 1.6 years behind in achievement when compared with children from intact homes (Guidubaldi et al., 1983, and Shinn, 1978). In the first few years of school, a large amount of skill-building takes place and new information is conveyed. Difficulty with concentration interferes with both academic skill-building and retention of new information. Most children learn to read, write, and perform basic mathematical calculations in the first, second, and third grades. These skills are foundations for learning and are difficult to master later in school. Academic difficulty impacts on the child's relationships and sense of self. Everyone in a classroom generally knows who is smart and who is "dumb"; once labeled "dumb," it is difficult to undo that reputation.

In a longitudinal study (Kelly & Wallerstein, 1976) of children whose parents divorced during this stage, sadness was the predominant feeling conveyed by the children. Children whose parents separated and divorced at an earlier chronological age were at less risk for sadness, although recent research (Wallerstein, 1985) suggests that some pervasive grief may always be present for children of divorce. Twenty years ago, many psychologists thought that children did not get depressed because they were rarely observed to sustain the same outer manifestations of depression as adults. In other words, children do not stop eating or become lethargic or verbalize extreme sadness as adults do when they are depressed. Today, however, it has been agreed that children do experience depression. The symptoms in children are usually ones of a depressed mood, self-effacing statements, lack of interest in activities and peers, and sometimes self-destructive or acting-out behaviors, such as stealing, fire setting, vandalism or behavior problems in school.

Depression in children is most often a reaction to some situational factor; rarely do children get depressed for no obvious reason. Loss of a parent, loss of a home environment, or overall change in the home environment are highly stressful events very likely to produce sadness and grief for all children of this age. Children who have no opportunity to resolve this grief are at high risk for depression. Children are more likely to grieve if those around them grieve, so it is crucial that parents do not hide their own distress or feelings of sadness about the divorce. This is not to say that children should be overwhelmed by a sense of their parents' sadness. Children have a strong need to know that someone is in control and to be assured that they will be provided with primary nurturance. As always, moderation is a key principle. Children need to remember and reminisce about how their home is different from the way it used to be, they need permission to feel an emptiness when there is an empty spot at the dinner table, and they need to be allowed to cry and feel sad. Children differ in the length of time they spend resolving their grief but, in general, six to nine months after the divorce, some diminishing of the sad feelings should be evident. After this amount of time, if the child still evidences feelings of despair or sadness that are intense or increasing, then professional help may be indicated.

Special Circumstances

While this book is arranged chronologically, it is not the chronological age of the child which is of primary concern to visitation arrangements; rather it is the developmental age which is crucial. A child may be seven years old but function psychologically more as a four year old. This may be true especially for children who are dealing with divorce, since regression (acting younger) is one of the common ways children cope with stress in their lives. Reading the sections on developmental issues for children of each age should help in determining whether your children are indeed dealing with the issues of their chronological age or whether they are still struggling with those of earlier ages. Each divorcing family is unique. Assessing your child's developmental stage, as well as patterns of attachment to the parents, is a crucial determinant in choosing the schedule of visitation with which to start. It is better to err in terms of using arrangements suggested for youngsters below your child's chronological age rather than using arrangements more suitable for older children.

For example, Matthew was a seven year old, only child. His parents had never married. When mother discovered her pregnancy, dad had expressed little interest in fathering a child. The mother decided to keep her baby and raise him; the father provided financial support to them both, but minimal visitation with Matthew occurred through the first three years of the child's life. At age three, the mother moved to the same city as the father, hoping to give her son some access to a father figure. Short visits took place for a couple of hours several times a month between Matthew and his father. Essentially, the father remained a stranger to Matthew while mother took on importance as the primary and sole psychological parent. When Matthew was seven, suddenly the father asked for greatly increased visitation. He wanted to have his son for overnights and weekends and to participate in his school and extracurricular activities. The mother, who previously thought she wanted a more involved father figure, was overwhelmed with anxiety about whether these visits were in her son's best interest. Unable to settle upon a reasonable visitation program for Matthew, the parents sought professional help in determining what Matthew was ready to handle psychologically in the way of visitation with his father.

This situation is not an unusual one. Some fathers cannot relate to the early child care roles of diapering, feeding, and frequent cuddling. They see these critical activities as "mothering" tasks. As their children grow older and less in need of such intensive care, these fathers begin to find it more gratifying to interact with the children. Individual personalities emerge with interests and hobbies. Suddenly these same fathers take a strong interest in their children and want to be a vital part of their lives.

It is easy to view these dads as undeserving. Why should they be allowed to move in at age six when their children are easier to care for and more enjoyable as individuals with whom to spend time? Mothers can understandably resent this transition; they feel that dad has not earned the right to a special relationship when it was mom who put in all the hard work prior to this time. Once again, it is important to emphasize that animosities must be put aside if the best interests of the children are to be served. What dad does or does not deserve may be a completely different issue than what is good for the child. Each situation must be judged on its own merits. It is suggested that a child deserves to receive whatever a parent is capable of giving, no matter how minimal, as long as the child is not harmed in the process. An opportunity to grow up feeling loved by both parents is a critical factor in healthy adaptation to adulthood. Dads, such as Matthew's, need to be allowed to participate in their children's lives.

Matthew was seven years old at the time of his father's renewed interest. Most seven year olds can move freely between their two parents' homes. Although he was seven years old chronologically, it was determined that Matthew had not progressed to a seven year old psychological relationship with his father. In fact, they had barely started to build a relationship; the two of them were struggling with the earliest relationship issues of building trust and attachment to each other. Consequently, the recommendations were that Matthew's visitation with his dad be similar to those in the developmental chart for the infant to two and one half year olds, in that Matthew and his dad were to start with short, frequent visits.

However, due to Matthew's age of seven years and greater emotional capacity, he could be expected to progress through the stages of relationship building at a much faster rate than it would take for a child to grow through the stages maturationally. It is advisable that parents begin with a visitation pattern appropriate to the emotional age of the relationship between the child and the parents. Progression through the stages should then occur fairly rapidly. A general guideline might be to move up one developmental stage every six to eight weeks as long as the relationship continues to be consistent and positive. Rapid movement through the recommended developmental guidelines necessitates talking with your children about their feelings and watching carefully for signs of regression or of anxiety. Should symptoms of either occur, slow down progression through the different patterns of visitation recommended for successive developmental stages. Psychologically healthy children usually can be expected to build relationships with their parents that are in line with their chronological ages within nine to twelve months.

Chapter Four:

"It's All Your Fault"
Nine to Twelve Years

Developmentally, nine to twelve year olds are focused on establishing proficiency in areas they began to master during earlier stages. These areas include peer relationships as well as athletic, academic, and artistic pursuits. Nine to twelve year olds are idealistic and enjoy the pride of being able to make genuine contributions to their community through participation in service organizations, church-related activities, and school extracurricular activities.

At this stage, the energies devoted to peer relationships focus on social organization and on fitting in with a valued group. Much attention is paid to appearance in general—i.e., clothing and grooming. Girls of this age are especially likely to note each detail of an envied peer's clothes, the way in which other girls carry their bodies and the signals displayed that indicate being "one of the popular girls." Frequently, there is a dichotomy between parental expectation and peer pressure. The nine to twelve year old must deal with this polarity on many levels. For example, David, age eleven, expressed conflict about having to choose between spending his time after school shooting baskets with his friends and maintaining involvement in the extracurricular activities carefully orchestrated by his well-intentioned mother and father.

Children of nine to twelve often define themselves by their subgroupings. While shifting alliances frequently, they experiment with different social roles. By this age, children have a performance history in areas of social, athletic, academic, and artistic skill building and they begin to identify and articulate their own strengths and weaknesses as compared to those of their peers.

Children of nine to twelve are able to care for their own basic needs related to food, clothing, and hygiene. At this point, children of divorce may handle their own telephone calls and communications with each parent. Parents who had difficulty in providing for basic needs when the child was in an earlier and more dependent stage may now find the relationship more rewarding and appealing. By nine to twelve years of age, children are able to participate fully in discussions. They have a vastly improved grasp of adult issues, including those surrounding their parents' divorce. They are not so likely to distort by means of magical thinking as younger children are. In fact, nine to twelve year olds tend to demand explanations. They characteristically express a great deal of empathic understanding of their parents' attitudes and reasons for divorce. They demand to know, and ultimately can understand why the divorce has taken place, and how they will be affected by resultant changes. The capacity for understanding also serves to heighten their awareness of their own vulnerability. Feelings of sadness, anger, and hurt are now clearly identifiable in the child. Wallerstein and Kelly (1976) point out that children ages nine to twelve often experience a sense of shame regarding the divorce; they tend to cover up their feelings of personal rejection when representing their situation to others. Their research indicated frequent disruptions of school performance as well.

Moreover, nine to twelve year olds are characterized by their idealism. At this level of maturity, they have incorporated many parental teachings of right and wrong, and they are increasingly competent to make moral judgments. Particularly in the divorce situation, their idealism easily can produce a sense of rage. This rage is frequently directed at the parent whose behavior the child identifies as at odds with his/her own sense of standards. The irony is that the child's standards are generally derived from the parents' teachings. For example, Tom, age twelve, displayed righteous indignation over the fact that his mother, acting in opposition to her prior teachings that families must stay together and work out their disagreements, had initiated a separation from his father. His personal sense of betrayal was very intense. Tom needed more specific information about the reasons for his mother's decision. Once he was given that, Tom's anger gave way to sadness and acceptance.

Residence and Visitation Recommendations
When both parents can maintain good functioning in the

parental role and they are willing, the nine to twelve year old is able to sustain relationships on an equal basis with each parent. Even if the caretaking arrangements have not been fifty-fifty up until this point, the child may be able to sustain alternating residence periods of one to two full weeks with each parent. A closeness may be achieved between the child and the parent with whom there has formerly been less contact. There is less need for constant replenishment of nurturing formerly provided by frequent contact with the primary parent.

It is extremely rare however that both parents are actually available and willing to parent fifty-fifty. One major requirement is that both parents must live close enough to provide equal access from both households to the same school, peers and activities. Parents need to be equally available to juggle issues of schedules and transportation from each household as well. These are necessary preconditions for a fully shared fifty-fifty custody arrangement.

Moreover, during this phase it becomes especially critical for the child to have input into the design of the residence and visitation pattern. Custody evaluators are aware that in stating their preference for residential parent, children in earlier developmental stages are more likely to select the parent who is needier, the one who the child senses is not coping as well and thus needs the child more. At nine to twelve years of age, children may state a preference for the more growth-fostering parent, the parent more likely to put his or her own needs aside in order to allow the child's needs to become primary.

Divorced parents of children at this developmental stage need to ask themselves honestly if their child's best interest will be served by a fifty-fifty split residential arrangement. There are many nine to twelve year olds who object to living on a fifty-fifty basis in two completely separate residences. Many children feel it is too confusing and burdensome to pack up and shift homes weekly. Many report losing a sense of belonging, losing a sense of feeling personally anchored with such a shift of homes, even though they are maintaining continuity in peer and community activities. Some people thrive on change—they are rare, and generally a desire for change is not typical of children. Frequently, parents are able to establish one residence as a "home base," while a weekly or monthly schedule of afternoons, evenings, and weekends are designated for the child to spend at the home of the other parent. It is important to establish living arrangements which have a predictable and stable pattern.

Another possible living arrangement is the "nesting" concept in which one complete household is maintained for the children and the parents take turns moving in and out. The major complication with this arrangement arises from the parent who experiences this as an invasion of privacy by the other parent. The adults may find it disruptive and difficult to organize their own work and recreational needs from two simultaneous home bases (giving, perhaps, some insight into what children in similar circumstances may be experiencing).

In situations where parents reside at great distances from each other, the nonresidential parent might consider spending time with the child one to three weekends per month as transportation conditions and financial circumstances permit. This, again, is best coordinated in conjunction with the youngster's input. In order to allow the maintenance of school and community involvement, it is advisable that for one or more of the weekend visits the nonresidential parent travel to where the child is enrolled in school.

Children state frequently that they want both their parents to observe them in activities and performances. Parents who reside at a distance might try to attend some of these events. Such involvement transmits the message that the parent cares about the child's increasing proficiencies. It is always recommended that the nonresidential parent establish direct relationships with the child's teachers, coaches, and other instructors rather than depend solely on the ex-spouse for information and access to these parts of a child's life. When one parent relies on the other parent to provide information regarding schedules, conferences and school reports, frequent complaints arise of inadequate information and intentional withholding. In all but the rarest instances this situation cultivates resentment and creates conflict between the parents.

Those parents who live too far from their children to participate in school and day-to-day functions might have additional visitation time which includes half of the two week Christmas vacation, all of the spring vacation, and Thanksgiving and President's Day weekends to avoid excessive interference with school activities. By nine to twelve years of age, summer visits may be extended from four to six weeks in one block of time. The well-functioning child can spend half the summer with each parent. Recommendations for maintaining the relationship between visits are elaborated further in Appendix C.

Risks

Difficulties encountered with the nine to twelve year old include the possibility that the child will build a very strong alliance with one parent against the other. Such an alliance potentially could develop into a long-standing disruption of the relationship between the other parent and the child, particularly in the situation where a child condemns the morality or behavior of one of the parents. A healthier resolution would be for the child to develop a tolerance for both parents' points of view and to receive the sanction of each parent to carry on a satisfactory relationship with the other parent.

While parents must communicate with the nine to twelve year old about their reasons for divorce, they must do so in a way which does not destroy the ability of the child to relate to one of the parents. While communicating about their own strengths and weaknesses, parents will want to impart a sense of their own coping capacities and avoid excessive blaming, discrediting, and denigrating of the other parent. Failing to do so encourages the child to act out against the opposite parent.

For example, the father of Allison, an eleven year old girl, had expressed confusion as to whether or not he should explain anything of the circumstances of the divorce to his child, who manifested declining interest in academic achievement as well as oppositional behavior at school. Allison was experiencing intense feelings of anger at her mother's apparent abandonment of her. Father, a conscientious parent, believed that he should never discuss anything about the motivations of the other parent with his child because of the risk that he would be discrediting the mother's parenting. The child, therefore, had no understanding of the conditions that led to her mother's initiating the divorce and moving away. When Allison was given some explanation of her mother's motivations, along with dad assuming his share of the responsibility for the breakup, she was more easily able to work through her angry feelings and resume healthy functioning.

Feelings of abandonment are a major contributing factor to a child's poor self-esteem. Children who feel a parent has abandoned them feel unloved and unlovable. Should a child develop this perception of being abandoned, the issue should be addressed by the parents, friends, or professionals.

As was the case for the six to eight year old children, when children of nine to twelve experience stress, it is commonly reflected in their school performance. They may demonstrate symptoms of aggression and oppositionalism throughout a readjustment period. It is important to keep lines of communication open and through discussion, help the child develop coping skills.

When relevant, the youngster may need occasional assistance from one parent in dealing with the other parent's weaknesses. For example, in one case where a dad upset his child by being consistently late at pick up times, mom needed to help her child understand that it was not the child's fault. When dad did not change his behavior as a result of the child talking about this concern, it was important for the child to understand that dad's chronic lateness was characteristic of dad and not a sign that the dad loved the child any less. Mom helped fortify the child's personal resources by sharing comments such as, "That is a part of your dad. You need to learn not to take it personally and to realize this is not a sign that dad doesn't love you." This mom found it necessary to remain detached from her own irritation with the situation in order to speak these words. She was helped in doing this by focusing on the goal of establishing a business-type relationship with her ex-spouse around raising their children.

Children of this age who view one of their parents as not coping well with the divorce may attempt to reverse roles in order to take over the parenting. Nine to twelve year olds are capable of tremendous understanding of the parent's point of view. During the post-divorce adjustment period, adults may appreciate and enjoy the fact that their children try to soothe them, express concern for their health, and worry about how they are coping. Nevertheless, a parent will serve the best interests of the child by assuring the youngster that the parent is capable of taking care of himself or herself as well as of the child, despite apparent sadness or temporarily poor functioning. This is not to suggest that a parent turn away all of a child's offerings of support and helpfulness. Rather, parents are advised to be sure that their children are proceeding with their own developmental tasks and that they have not withdrawn interest in peer relations and community activities in favor of playing the caretaker role at home.

For example, Diane, age ten, withdrew from peers and focused her attention on making certain her mother was well fed and taken care of. She expressed considerable concern about how well her mother was coping. This worry occupied her thoughts, focusing her away from school work and preventing her from functioning academically and socially. In another instance, Paul, age twelve, would endlessly ingratiate himself and lie so as to not upset his residential parent, his father. Recognizing his dependency on this parent, Paul expressed dire concern about the negative effects on his dad's health that any additional stress might bring. Paul attempted to camouflage his own difficulties to avoid being the source of any further stress to his dad.

Special Circumstances

Studies of children conducted five to ten years after a divorce (Wallerstein, 1983) indicate that children who cope best are those who have maintained a continuing relationship with both of their parents. Even when a parent remarries and forms a new family, that parent remains just as emotionally significant to the child. When children are asked many years after a divorce to describe themselves or to draw pictures of their families, they do not depict themselves as coming from a single parent. Almost uniformly, children of divorce think of themselves as having two parents, even though these two parents reside in different homes. It is all too rare that the parents in an intact family set aside time to spend with each child individually. Parent-child relations may become diffused and diminished by the variety of disruptions that occur in a family. Interestingly, the relationship between parent and child has the potential to grow in importance following a divorce because of the increased potential for one-to-one sharing.

One family arrived at an unusual arrangement that capitalized on the assets each parent had to offer their child. These parents recognized that the disruption caused by their inability to communicate with each other was impacting negatively on their elementary school-aged daughter. Their communications with each other were bitter and angry. With the help of a mediator, they were able to identify and define very specifically and concretely the parenting strengths each had to offer. As a result of mediation, the father assumed responsibility for all decisions in the area of the child's education, while the mother assumed responsibility for decisions related to extracurricular activities. The parents selected jointly a single medical doctor and agreed they would each utilize this physician, notifying the other in writing of any medical services provided for their child. They agreed as well not to communicate with each other except through the third party mediator. While this might sound like an extreme and untenable solution, it turned out to be a very workable arrangement, one that greatly improved the quality of the relationship between each parent and their daughter. The arrangement was successful in reducing the psychological distress suffered by all members of this family from the formerly bitter and angry exchanges among them.

Although continual fighting between parents is likely to interfere with developmental progress for children at all ages, children of later elementary school age have a complicating risk. These children are more likely to take sides. Their anger about the divorce is intense, well-organized and likely to become directed at one parent if continual fighting between parents creates such an opportunity. These youngsters are prone to jump into the battle by strongly aligning themselves with one parent and vehemently directing their anger towards the other. When this occurs, the risk of impairing the relationship with one parent for a prolonged period is heightened.

Another caution should be noted for children of elementary school age. Children overhear far more than adults generally think they do. Parents frequently share their economic, psychological and health concerns over the phone or in person with family and friends. While adults are conversing, children may appear to be playing happily or to be intently engaged in a television program. The parent mistakenly may assume a private conversation is taking place. It is more likely that the child is acutely aware of what the parent is relating about their family and life circumstances. This personal information is far more interesting and important to the child than play or T.V. Psychologists find that children can report in great detail conversations that they have overheard. But while children may hear the concrete details being relayed, they may fail to understand the context and intent of the communication. Children, instead, jump to their own conclusions and often assume that the issue being discussed involves them. Particularly during the initial stages of divorce, children are generally stressed, frightened, and hurting. Their sense of vulnerability causes them to react self-protectively. This is not quite the same phenomenon as the "magical thinking" of a preschool-aged child but it does stem from a similar self-centered interpretation of the world.

For example, Jill, age nine, had seen a physician for trouble with curvature of the spine and also had been found to need braces on her teeth. Simultaneously, she became aware of her recently divorced parents' continual arguing about money. The concurrence of these medical necessities with her parents' arguments about money led her to conclude that she was at fault for their disagreements. Jill's worrying led to increasing problems with her body image, decreased feelings of self-worth and attractiveness. When the parents became aware of the impact their bickering was having on their daughter, they were able to greatly limit their combative behavior. Very quickly, Jill's self-image began to improve and she was able to speak in a manner reflecting increased positive self-esteem and confidence about her attractiveness.

Chapter Five:

"I'm Dropping Out"
Thirteen to Eighteen Years

Developmental Tasks

The adolescent's tasks are many but they all center around one theme: emancipation. The adolescent is preparing to leave home and is working toward establishing a sense of self as separate from the family. In order to successfully accomplish emancipation, adolescents must psychologically detach from their parents. Normally, the process of separation consists of a gradual trying out of different roles which may be accompanied by mood swings that range from intense joy to horrendous pain. The struggle is most often a lonely one. Adolescents often suffer silently, pushing other family members away. Yet, much like one to two and one half year old children, adolescents have a deep need to be reassured that they are loved in spite of being separate. In other words, they need to refuel from time to time. The family unit is the base from which teenagers gain sustenance and a belief in themselves before the next venture away.

Generally, the earlier adolescent years are the ones in which the greatest amount of emotional work takes place. The tasks of emancipation can be understood more easily if categorized into individual steps. It is important to understand that all the steps toward emancipation actually occur simultaneously. There are ebbs and flows within each step as the individual adolescent works toward emancipation. The developmental steps toward emancipation are (1) solidifying a sense of self and of separate identity; (2) mourning the loss of childhood, dependency, and the sense of protection found within the family unit; (3) learning to handle sexual feelings effectively with the ultimate goal of establishing a long-term intimate relationship; (4) learning to balance impulse discharge with the rules of society. (Blos, 1979).

Adolescence is a stage where there are enormous emotional demands, a time during which young people act as if they have little need for parental support. In actuality, it is probably as crucial to have parental support during adolescence as it was during the first three years of life. Some people falsely believe that adolescents are not affected by divorce and that this, therefore, is an acceptable time to dissolve the family unit. According to research findings (Wallerstein & Kelly, 1976; Sorosky, 1977), this conception is untrue. Young teenagers experience extraordinary pain when their parents divorce. Although they are in distress, they usually will not show this in an obvious way; nor will they talk about it. Adolescents often try to act as if they can handle anything. If asked to share their feelings about an impending divorce, they may shrug their shoulders and announce that "it isn't any big deal" and they really don't care what their parents want to do. The data suggest otherwise.

Children of this age need to react to an existing family unit in order to work through the emotional detachment process. When parents divorce prior to the youngsters' completion of this process, the emotional message to adolescents is that their family has given them up before they had the chance to work through giving up the family. As the family dissolves, the adolescent may experience feelings of abandonment. How can the adolescent detach from something that is falling apart or seemingly nonexistent? The result is that there is interference with a crucial phase of emancipation, namely mourning the loss of the family. The family is no longer the same one to which the child bonded and attached as a young child. The changed family unit causes a reaction of either an abrupt halt to the emancipation process or an accelerated detachment from the family. Either way, the process of detaching slowly, at his or her own pace, is no longer possible for the adolescent. It also may mean that there is no home base from which to refuel.

At least temporarily, adults are very disrupted by divorce. It is not uncommon for parents of teenagers to expect moral support, increased independence, and comforting for themselves from their teenager at the time of the divorce. Parents are usually emotionally depleted and may have lowered reserves left for giving. As previously mentioned, the teenager is the last one to admit to being needy. A stance of pseudo-maturity or fierce independence is likely to mislead parents into believing that the child needs less support than is actually the case. Wallerstein and Kelly's (1974) study of divorcing families revealed that the manner in which parents handled the divorce was more crucial to a child's psychological well-being during the adolescent years than during the earlier years. Parents who (1) stayed involved with and continued to nurture their teenager, (2) did not themselves start acting like adolescents, and (3) maintained consistent boundaries and limits on impulse control fostered an environment in which the developmental task of emancipation could continue to take place successfully.

Interestingly, families that were able to create such an atmosphere often found that initially their teenagers withdrew from them. Many young teenagers appear to cope with divorce by staying far away from the battleground, by psychologically withdrawing themselves, and appearing as if they already have mastered detachment. Later, when the parents have settled into two separate family units, the teenager emotionally returns to more active engagement with both parents and demonstrates renewed capacity for emotional expression. This coping strategy might be labeled as a form of strategic withdrawal. Healthy, well-functioning teenagers may temporarily remove themselves emotionally from the family unit. When the greatest time of distress has passed, they return to finish the psychological work of emancipation.

Residence and Visitation Recommendations

It is essential that teenagers have some say and participation in planning related to their own lives. As a natural consequence of the emancipation process, they will resist and resent situations that are thrust upon them. This, however, does not mean that adolescents should make the rules for their living arrangements or visitation patterns. Rather, it is important that their feelings and input be considered and heavily weighed in any final decision.

Adolescents encountering a parental divorce tend toward two very different reactions. Each is deserving of a separate discussion because each response raises different problems for residence and visitation planning. As discussed earlier, adolescents may remove themselves from the battleground entirely. Often divorce accelerates the detachment process. Adolescents begin to view their parents in a more differentiated and accurate way than was previously possible. No longer dependent solely on their parents, teenagers are able to step back and see the strengths and weaknesses within each parent with amazing astuteness. At the onset of a divorce, it is not uncommon to find young adolescents functioning in a healthier fashion psychologically than their parents. These well-adjusted adolescents are easily identifiable by their resistance to taking sides, their ability to appraise each of the adults, and their feeling of a sense of self as separate from the parents.

Chances are great that these adolescents will have an understanding of what each parent can offer and will request residence and visitation arrangements that allow for their needs to be met. For example, one parent may allow greater pursuit of social activities, more access to peers, or more opportunity to pursue a hobby or interest. The adolescent will ask for enough contact with that parent to have these needs met. Most adolescents are in the midst of concentrating on their own sexual feelings and their sense of themselves as male or female. Usually, they prefer to have the greatest contact, and frequently their home base, with the parent of the same sex, but sometimes not.

As a rule, adolescents seem more aligned to their peer groups than to their families. The concentration on peers is one of the primary mechanisms used to detach psychologically from parents. Therefore, social and peer needs will play a large role in their choices. The parent who continues living in close proximity to peers and out-of-school activities may well be the choice for a home base. The parent living some distance away may refer to Appendix C for suggestions on maintaining a long-distance relationship with a teenager.

Another common reaction in adolescents facing the divorce of their parents is absolute fury at one parent along with over-idealization of the other parent. Adolescents who respond in this mode often stand in judgment of what has precipitated the divorce; they take sides, and bitterly express their anger at the parent they view as at fault. Such anger may become so entrenched that it disorganizes the child for a period of time. Teenagers with such entrenched anger may refuse to have any contact or visitation with the parent being scapegoated. Obviously, children of this age cannot be forced into visitation if they steadfastly refuse. It is unwise, however, to allow them to seriously compromise the relationship with one of their parents. A short cooling off period is acceptable; but during that time, the parent receiving the hostility and blame should continue to express his or her interest in and love for the child. If within a period of about eight to twelve weeks, feelings have not settled enough for the child to be more amenable to re-establish contact with that parent, then some professional help is urged to help uncover the underlying reasons why the youngster's anger has become so chronically entrenched.

Children who cut off contact with one of their parents are often regretful in later life. A decision to terminate contact with one parent or the other is usually based on an earlier, unresolved problem within the parent-child relationship. This needs exploration and understanding. If a teenager chooses to reject having a relationship with a parent after gaining insight into his or her reasons for such a decision, then the potential for future psychological problems and pathology for that individual will be far less.

In general, adolescents are best served by living arrangements into which they have had a large amount of input. At this age, fully shared custody or joint physical custody is very much a real possibility. Moving back and forth between homes is not as disruptive as it is to the younger child. Adolescents can make use of the phone, of public transportation, and of peer relationships in order to maintain contact with both parents and with their outside activities.

To avoid enabling too great a possibility for impulsive, on-the-spot decision making, it is wisest to establish a permanent schedule with some degree of flexibility built in. Teenagers should not be allowed to move back and forth between two homes to suit their own whims or to avoid dealing with troublesome rules or limitations at one home by fleeing to the other. Almost any arrangement is possible, from having a home base with one parent and visitation on regularly scheduled days with the other parent, to a split living arrangement, with three days up to two weeks, at one home and the remaining time at the other. Whatever the schedule, it should be clear that the arrangements are firm. Flexibility should be reasonably allowed to meet special circumstances, such as school or peer functions that are more easily participated in from one home than the other. It is important to remember that although a great deal of parental control has been given up at this stage, the parent still must make the rules.

If a reasonable plan, which takes the needs of the teenager into account, has been set up and the plan is being abused so that one or both parents are feeling manipulated, it may be time to seek professional help. If a plan has been in effect for some time, it may be important to consider revising it. Emotional growth through the adolescent years is enormous. What the child's stated needs were at age thirteen and what they may be at age sixteen can be worlds apart.

For example, Christopher, a young adolescent preferred a living arrangement similar to his earlier childhood years, namely making his home with his mother. By middle adolescence, Christopher preferred living with the same-sex parent and had far less concern around basic dependency needs and more concern around gender identification.

As a general rule, it has been recommended throughout this book that living and visitation patterns be revised every three years. Such revision may need to be applied more frequently for the adolescent, possibly as often as yearly. While enormous emotional growth spurts can take place during adolescence, lags in emotional growth are not uncommon either. Being open-minded and receptive to revisions is essential as long as the revisions are not taking place so frequently that the parents are being manipulated by the teenager.

Risks

Progressing through the adolescent years presents risk under the best of circumstances. When the adolescent period is affected by a family breakup, either in this stage or a previous one, the risk of interference with development is increased.

Following a divorce, adults commonly behave in an adolescent fashion themselves. They are moody, depressed, have a need to re-establish some sense of identity, and often become more openly sexual to affirm their attractiveness. Previously parents provided a sense of stability, seemed to be in control, and exercised restraints and good judgment. Suddenly they are in distress themselves and may even turn to the adolescent to receive comforting.

Not only have the teenagers lost the security of a clear boundary between parent and child, they may have to contend with the fact that their parents are sexual beings as well. All through childhood, children commonly deny their parents' sexuality. It is ordinarily something that they successfully repress, even when events such as the birth of a sibling confirm that the parents have an active sexual relationship. When parents begin to date, children are forced into an awareness of their parents' sexuality. Such awareness usually stirs up an enormous amount of discomfort for adolescents who are just learning to manage their own sexual feelings and considering the possibility of a future intimate relationship. Many young teenagers attempt to manage their sexual anxiety by regressing to an earlier level of psychological development. They try to deny their own sexuality by remaining immature and by vowing never to marry.

When divorce occurs during adolescence, it takes a great toll on the ability of a child to trust in the lasting nature of relationships. At the very time that adolescents are struggling to define what matters within a relationship, who can be trusted to love and value them, and what sustains a relationship, these children are witnessing the failure of the primary model they have had for conceptualizing male-female relationships. The result may be a fear reaction. Teenagers may become terrified that they will have the same outcome befall them as happened to their parents, and thus vow never to have a relationship and become so vulnerable.

One of the hardest tasks for both parents and children is learning to believe in relationships again. When one has been badly hurt, it takes a long healing period before one is ready to take a chance in trusting once more, knowing this time that there are no forevers. Teenagers differ in the impact such hurt has on them but almost all report tremendous concern about their own ability to sustain and maintain a relationship (Sorosky, 1977). Some youngsters withdraw for many years. They do not date or express an interest in their appearance, and they avoid situations which place them in contact with the opposite sex. Others initiate frantic activity to prove that they are still lovable. They may develop an all-encompassing relationship with a boyfriend or girlfriend, such that they can hardly bear to have their love object out of their sight. They may take inordinate risks, and sacrifice other aspects of their life in order to maintain this intimate relationship. Still other teenagers may act out promiscuously in an attempt to feel loved (Hetherington, 1972; Kalter, 1977).

Both parents need to communicate clearly that they still love and care for their child even though they have chosen to no longer live in the original nuclear family. This is not always easy to communicate to teenagers who resist overtures of affection as childish and embarrassing. The parents must make special time for giving attention to their child's interests: attending events and engaging in conversations without probing or bringing up topics of conflict. Acts of continued nurturance are effective ways to express continued love for the child at this difficult age. Teenagers are best assured that they are still worthy of being loved when they are able to maintain free access to and contact with both of their parents.

Some adolescents cope with divorce by substituting a new family for the one they lost. These are the children who turn to various subgroups, such as religious or drug subcultures, in order to define a sense of belonging. The adolescents who take this course transfer their strong needs for a sense of identity, structure, values, and limit setting to a group other than their nuclear family. They find a new family to belong to that now sets the standards for their behavior. This chosen path for coping is probably one of the most alarming because it represents withdrawal from the family unit. While some teenagers eventually emancipate from such subgroups, rejoining the larger world and renewing a relationship with their parents at a later age, some never resolve their differences.

All parents need to be watchful for signs that their adolescents are not mastering successfully the developmental tasks of this stage. Adolescents may become overwhelmed by the additional stress imposed by a divorce. Parents need to do all they can to remain available to communicate with their adolescents. Seeking outside help at the earliest sign of trouble is the best avenue for preventing problems that may escalate into serious threats to an adolescent's physical or emotional well being.

Special Circumstances

Each case of adolescent visitation and living arrangements represents special circumstances. Successful visitation requires that the input from the adolescent be considered seriously along with a commitment from both parents and adolescents to make the plan work.

For example, Rebecca, age fourteen, continually denied her feelings of anger and discomfort about being caught in the middle between her feuding parents. She was the older of two children, somewhat reserved socially, and dedicated to her studies. Although pleasant and engaging with adults, she had always been content to stay home, functioning on the periphery of peer social involvement. When Rebecca's parents separated, they decided to establish separate residences within close proximity. Throughout the ensuing months, they continually tried out new residence and visitation arrangements for Rebecca, changing them frequently as they perceived their own needs to be shifting. There was periodic talk of reconciliation, which never came to fruition. In the same period of time, Rebecca abandoned her schoolwork, which had been her mainstay in elementary and early junior high. She became involved with peers, at first with the approval of her parents who saw this socializing as long in coming. The peer group she chose, however, enjoyed staying out late, going to parties at a local college campus, coming home appearing to be drunk or not coming home at all. At first Rebecca experienced enhanced social competency and elation. These feelings rapidly gave way to depression and dismay when several of her friends were involved in an alcohol-related car accident in which serious injuries occurred. Only then was Rebecca able to step back, assess her position, and come to grips with her feelings of intense disappointment and anger about her parents' apparent lack of direction which she perceived as having destroyed her home and her sense of stability. These parents finally determined to live apart, and they settled on a permanent residence and visitation plan which considered their daughter's input. Rebecca's unhealthy behavior pattern and feelings of anger and instability diminished considerably.

Brent, age eighteen, angry with his father for seeking a divorce, had refused contact with him for three years. His dad, feeling distant and estranged, had relied on mom to bring up the children. Continuing a pattern which had lasted throughout the couple's marriage, the mother was the primary mediator between the father and his three children. At the point that therapy was initiated for this family, the dad was afraid to approach Brent, perceiving him as fragile psychologically. Throughout the divorce, mother had relied heavily on Brent's emotional support. Dad moved away at a time when Brent had been experimenting with drugs and had been involved in some petty criminal activity. His father had voiced strong disapproval, even condemnation of Brent and his lifestyle. Needless to say, dad also had a long list of complaints against mom, the most important of which was his perception that she had always withheld affection. When dad moved away, Brent entered into a strong coalition against his father by siding with his embittered mother. Simultaneously, he dropped out of school and became increasingly isolated. In the context of family therapy, his dad was able to come to grips with his own style of withholding affection. He recognized that his personal focus had estranged him from his family over the years, that it was not all his ex-wife's undermining of him in his relationship with his son as he had originally perceived. He arrived at a point where he was able to express his love and concern for his son directly and openly. Initially, he shared this with him in a letter. This became the first step towards more normalized communication. Out of this an increasing sense of trust grew. Soon after, Brent returned to high school and came to rely on his father for consultation in his own career direction. By his early twenties, he had given up his self-destructive behavior and had established himself in a career path. The important point to note is that the parent is generally the one who must do the reaching out and resolving of communication impasses which leave one parent mistrusted, misunderstood, and scapegoated in the family.

Kimberly was thirteen years old when her father and mother separated. At first, things worked out relatively well for Kimberly. She continued to attend the same school where she was well-known and well-liked. She lived alternating weeks with her dad in the old neighborhood and with her mom and new step-father who had moved across town. The mother provided Kimberly with transportation to and from school on those days when she was in residence with her. After a few months, Kimberly's mother started expressing her need to move to another state with her new husband to support his career. Kimberly expressed feelings of helplessness, of being torn apart, but to no avail. Mom felt determined to make the move and to try to sustain a relationship with Kimberly over the miles. By the start of the next school year, her mom and her step-father had relocated out of state, promising Kimberly that they would stay in close touch, fly in to be with her frequently, and call her several times a week. Mom was unable to sustain these promises. Over the months, Kimberly's behavior began to deteriorate. She began to skip classes, dress in extreme and unusual ways, and was vague in accounting for her whereabouts. Her behavior escalated to defiance of teachers and noncompliance with authority at school and at home. Ultimately, Kimberly's father brought her to therapy, exasperated because he was unable to control his formerly docile and approval-seeking daughter. She recently had been suspected of vandalizing the girls' restroom at school and had been involved in an incident of provocation at a local shopping mall. In therapy, Kimberly melted into tears when describing the hurt from her mom's perceived abandonment of her. Kimberly expressed a longing to live with her mom, but a fear that her dad might then not maintain a long distance relationship with her should she tell him that she wished to change her residence. In the following sessions, it was resolved that at the end of the school year, a change of residence would take place. Kimberly and her father painstakingly and in great detail worked out their intended long-distance communication by telephone and mail, and scheduled trips as well. Toward the end of the school year, Kimberly became increasingly reassured and demonstrated greater ability to verbalize her feelings of rage at the injustice of her parents' separation, rather than act them out. Her dad was able to maintain his contact as promised over the next school year and Kimberly began to function once again in a socially acceptable and more stable manner.

Questions and Answers

The following questions and answers span developmental levels. The questions have been frequently asked by divorced or divorcing parents. As you read them, you will find the various questions to be of greater or lesser significance to you and your situation. The format of this section allows for selective reading of important or relevant topic areas.

Table of Contents

Q: What about parents who reconcile?

Most children never stop dreaming and hoping that their parents will reconcile. Wallerstein (1985) completed a ten year follow-up of children who were originally studied when their parents divorced. Over eighty percent of these young people continued to report sorrow around the divorce and a sense of having missed out on something tremendously important by not having had an intact family during their growing-up years. Most of the individuals, including those who had grown into adulthood, said their strongest desire through childhood was that their parents would get back together again. The wish persisted for all age groups, even after reality told them that reconciliation clearly was not possible.

Some children actively manipulate to try to get their parents to reconcile; other children fantasize and wish. Those who accept that reconciliation will never happen experience a sadness and a mourning for the original family that never totally dissipates.

When parents do reconcile, it is like a dream come true. Young children, at the stage characterized by magical thinking, frequently believe they caused the reconciliation by wishing very hard for it to happen or behaving in some superstitious way. Older children may believe they somehow manipulated it and thus are left with a tremendous sense of power and control.

One example of a case of reconciliation that resulted in an experience of loss for a child involved Ethan, age six. Ethan was brought to therapy manifesting considerable behavior problems following his parents' reconciliation. For Ethan, the parents' reuniting represented a loss, especially of his father. While his parents lived separately, there was an identifiable visitation time with dad. When the parents reconciled, because of their newly rekindled romantic relationship, they spent time almost exclusively with each other. The father withdrew his one-to-one availability from the child. Ethan began to long for the special parenting he had received when he was involved in a fixed visitation schedule with each parent. Thus, ironically, reconciliation is not always a problem-free situation, nor an easy solution. While children will be relieved that their parents have come back together, they may painfully experience the loss of their previous relationship with each parent. All parents might gain from recognizing the fact that children tend to benefit from special identifiable times with each parent.

One of the saddest things for a child is when parents reconcile and then later divorce again. The effect on children is that they no longer know what to believe in or what to trust. One thing children need to have while growing up is a belief that their parents are there for them to trust. When they are told things are one way and then the situation turns out to be another way, children feel they have been betrayed.

Q: At each age level, how much weight should be given to the children's opinions about how much time they would like to spend with each parent?

As soon as children can verbalize, their preferences should be considered. Parents should try to understand their children's points of view. Residence and visitation schedules need to be revised at least every three years and possibly more frequently as developmental needs change. Decisions to revise should be made by the parents, taking their children's wishes into consideration.

For the most part, children are not comfortable making final decisions about which parent they are going to be with or what the visitation schedule is going to be. It is reassuring for children to know that their input will be considered but that the parents will make the actual decisions and work out the details. Parental decision making takes the weight off the youngsters' shoulders by not forcing them into loyalty binds or forcing them to choose between parents.

Q: What should parents do when their children request a change in their visitation schedule? For example, an older child, who is scheduled to spend the major portion of the summer with dad, suddenly says, "I don't want to spend that much time away from my friends. I don't want to go for the whole summer to another state to visit."

If a child does not want to visit the other parent, it is important to listen to the reasons why. Are there indications that fear, threat or abuse are a concern? If the parents cannot communicate about the visitation problem in a reasonable way, then an outside party, such as a mediator, therapist, social worker, even a trusted friend or a minister, can be asked to help give the parents constructive feedback.

Sometimes children will say one thing to one parent and another thing to the other parent. They may express to dad, "I would like to spend more time with you. I wish I could visit for longer." Then, they come home to mom and say, "I would like to shorten my visits with dad to spend more time with you." The younger the child is, the more likely a parent is to hear some of these contradictory views. Generally, the older children get, the more weight one should give to their input. But never should children alone decide what their visits will be. This is too much responsibility for a child to have. Parents should listen to their children to find out why they might be expressing a desire to change or modify their visitation, but ultimately the parents must be responsible for the decision.

It is important for mom and dad to understand that a teenager might suddenly tell a parent, "I don't want to spend the whole summer with you." This statement may be motivated by the adolescent's changing developmental needs rather than a reflection of the quality of the relationship between the parent and the child. The task of later childhood is one of emancipation, of detaching emotionally from the family. It is a normal, healthy part of being at this stage for children to desire to stay in an environment with their friends, to take a summer job, or to go to summer camp and be apart from the family. Giving children permission to start detaching as they are ready in middle and late adolescence encourages normal and healthy psychological development.

Q: *What if a child does not want to go on a specific, regularly scheduled visit?*

This comes up fairly often. A child will suddenly cry, plead, or ask not to go on a regularly scheduled visit. But children should go unless they have an illness or some very important pre-arranged plans, such as a special holiday or a birthday party of a very good friend. On the whole, it makes children feel too burdened with responsibility to regulate their own visits. When children are given too much decision-making power, they come, over time, to feel vulnerable, frightened, and overwhelmed. Parents are viewed as protectors and ultimate decision makers in keeping a child's world safe. Allowing your child to assume too much of this adult role will result in underlying feelings of helplessness and fear.

Parents may be reassured to know that sometimes children will go out the door crying and in tears, yet surprisingly within ten or fifteen minutes they will be fine. Fathers and mothers have reported that frequently within minutes "she quit crying and all was fine." Parents might well keep in mind that children are experiencing a painful loss of one parent as well as reunion with the other during transitions. Children may be helped immensely during transitions by prior planning of a special re-entry activity. As previously suggested, looking forward to the preparation of a special dinner, playing a designated game, or entertaining a special friend or relative upon returning home often helps ease the loneliness that may accompany transition.

Sometimes a reluctance to visit may stem from the kind of arrangement being made for the child. Parents need to check the developmental chart for the recommendations for children of each age. Care should be taken not to push the child into arrangements which are too advanced developmentally.

Q: When a parent lives out of state, wouldn't it be better to have one extended visit, such as an entire summer, than to only see that away parent once or twice a year for a brief time?

The visitation recommendations for younger children are that they have short but frequent visits with the non-residential parent. For an out-of-state parent, this recommendation can be expensive. Often parents say it would be easier and cheaper to send their four year old to dad for the whole summer. These parents feel they cannot afford to arrange short, frequent visitations. Although the recommended approach to visitation may initially cost parents more money or make life for parents more difficult, there is little doubt about the emotional and psychological benefits of these arrangements for the young child. If pushed prematurely into long visitations, young children, not yet ready for lengthy stays away from their home environment, may not show immediate signs of distress. Visible symptoms eventually will become obvious, however, when children are being pushed beyond their capacity to cope. The risks of advancing children prematurely into visitation patterns that they are not yet ready to handle are elaborated in each chapter. For parents who cannot afford short, frequent visits out of state, Appendix C lists many alternative techniques for maintaining a relationship across a long distance.

Q: What are some of the possible long-term effects of divorce on children?

Divorce is a common phenomenon. It is estimated that as many as 50 to 60 percent of all children will be affected by divorce (U.S. News and World Report, 1986). Adults may remember children they knew in school whose parents were divorced. These children stood out as unique because it was unusual for people to get divorced. You, yourself might have been a child of divorce. If so, you will probably remember that it was a difficult subject about which to talk and that few resources were available to help. Perhaps you felt very isolated and different.

Some of our knowledge about the effects of divorce on children comes from adults who have been in therapy. One woman in her early thirties came into therapy because she experienced confusion about not having a solid value system. Her parents had divorced when she was in early adolescence. There was diminished parenting capacity, availability, and support from her parents. Following the divorce, she became extremely alienated from her peers and continued to struggle with identity issues even into adulthood. Eventually, she adopted religious values, never offered by her parents, which gave her enough anchoring to feel that she could maintain a purposeful direction in her life. From the time of her parents' divorce, she had doubted herself and felt as if she lacked meaning and direction.

Another adult woman who came into therapy had experienced her parents' divorce at age five. Their divorce was extremely bitter and the custody battle over her continued well into her adolescence. This woman displayed many symptoms of early stress and developmental delays. She was a dependent adult with low self-esteem who required constant emotional reassurance from others. While it may be unfair to conclude that all the problems of her dependency in adulthood were the direct result of the divorce, she clearly retained intrusive and disturbing memories of the divorce interfering with her childhood.

The experience of a parental divorce for a child of any age is almost without exception a significant emotional event. The effects may be carried into adulthood if not worked out during childhood. It is the loss and rejection aspects of divorce that most often carry potentially disrupting effects into adulthood. Minimizing the losses a child experiences during a divorce can reduce the long-range consequences.

Q: What if one parent feels that the other parent is too permissive? For instance, one parent says, "When my children visit with the other parent, they eat fast foods, they do not go to church on Sunday, and there is no bedtime set for them." How seriously should complaints such as these be taken?

The psychological benefits that children accrue from maintaining a relationship with each parent in their lives is far more important than how permissive either parent may be. If, however, while visiting at the other parent's home, the children are actually endangered because that other parent is too disturbed or distracted to supervise adequately, then complaints are valid and warranted. Except for these instances, the relationship with the other parent should take precedence over the fact that lifestyles and values may be different at each parent's home.

This tenet may be very difficult to accept, to integrate and to understand. The fact is, if the parents had the same values and chose the same lifestyles, they would likely not have divorced in the first place. Even parents living under the same roof have different values and sometimes different rules. Children can understand and live with this situation. One of the hardest lessons for parents to learn in a divorce is that they must give up total control over their children. They inherently give up almost all control while the children are visiting at the other parent's home.

Q: Does a parent have the right to set rules about behavior at the other parent's home?

One mother expressed concern because while visiting their father's house, her daughters, ages seven and nine, would walk to school unsupervised. The father was aware of his ex-spouse's concern and felt that he was not being negligent, rather that the mother was unduly concerned about the children. The father believed that the girls' unsupervised five or six block walk to school not only would build their sense of self-esteem but also their sense of mastery and accomplishment. He had carefully considered the pros and cons of sending them by themselves. It was not something he was allowing or encouraging without thoughts of the children's well-being.

One morning as the children were preparing to go to school, the girls said, "Mom told us that we are not allowed to go to school alone from your house." This father was irate. He viewed it as the neighborhood norm to walk to school, as other children of these ages were allowed to do. The mother, on the other hand, felt that this represented an endangering situation for her youngsters. Her primary worry seemed to be that her girls might be assaulted, kidnapped or harmed in some way while unsupervised. She felt that the father provided extremely poor judgment by allowing his children to do this.

These are dad's kids, too. The way he raises the girls, the lifestyle and values at his home are his. Mother must learn, if dad is a well-functioning parent, to yield to his judgment when the children are in his care. She does have a right, however, to express her opinions and to express her concerns to dad, directly or through a neutral third party or mediator. Similarly, dad has the responsibility to consider the concerns she expresses. In this example, while the mom had reason for concern, dad was exercising his best judgment and ultimately he reassured mom that his home did not represent an endangerment to the children. Children report feeling caught in the middle when they are made to be responsible for conveying the rules to one parent which have been made by the other parent.

Q: What should be done if children report fearful feelings about visitation at one parent's home?

It is essential to uncover what has made the children feel fearful. Chances are they will share this information with someone they trust. The reasons may range from seeing a parent appear to be out of control while extremely angry to being physically or sexually abused by the parent or actually seeing the parent draw a weapon. Indeed, if the fear-inducing reason represents an endangerment, it is time to seek professional consultation about whether or not visitation should continue to occur at that parent's home. If the child is not safe left alone with the parent, supervised visits may be necessary. This means that another responsible adult is required to be present during the parent/child visits. Ordinarily in these instances, a mental health professional decides at what point that parent is ready to assume independent visitation. Supervised visitation services are provided in most communities either privately or in local hospitals, mental health centers, or other social service organizations.

Under these circumstances, parents are advised to contact a lawyer. Furthermore, they must contact their local department of social services if they suspect physical or sexual abuse is occurring during visits to the opposite parent's home. The department of social services is required to conduct an independent evaluation to assess whether the suspected abuse can indeed be confirmed. If abuse is confirmed, the residence and/or visitation arrangements will need to be modified legally to assure the safety and well-being of the children.

Physical endangerment is much easier for a professional to assess than psychological endangerment, which is when a child is at some emotional risk while at the other parent's home. Parents often complain about psychological endangerment. For instance, a mother might say, "When my child returns from visits with his dad, he seems hurt emotionally." Sometimes a parent complains that the children are being hurt emotionally because the other parent lives according to different values. Sometimes a parent feels their children are being psychologically endangered because the other parent sets standards that are very high, is extremely critical, or attempts to involve the children in activities which are beyond their capacity. Or it may be that mom or dad goes away for the weekend leaving the children with a sitter or at a friend's home.

This is a complex issue. A parent is harmful to a child psychologically when there is evidence demonstrating that while spending time with that parent the child is overly stressed, fearful, anxious, at risk of physical, sexual, or excessive verbal abuse. This is a very different concept from the existence of differing parental values. Parents not attending the same church, not preparing the same kinds of meals, not setting the same bedtime limits are not necessarily damaging to the child psychologically.

The major difficulty in assessing emotional abuse is that psychological damage may not be visible immediately as physical abuse is likely to be; however, in the long run it may be even more devastating. Therefore, concerns about emotional endangerment warrant serious consideration. Parents need to inventory their own feelings in order to judge whether they are looking for ammunition against the opposite parent or whether they are worried about the welfare of their children. If they are legitimately worried, an outside evaluator should be consulted in order to determine if emotional abuse is occurring.

Q: What can be done when there are continuing communication problems between the parents?

It is difficult to put animosity aside following a divorce. Therefore it sometimes becomes impossible for one parent to hear something from the other parent about the children even if it is a reasonable and logical idea or suggestion.

Often children are the only potent weapon that one parent can use against the other parent. Sometimes a parent feels so angry and hurt that he/she would like to withhold the children just so that other parent will hurt as much as he/she does. Many parents say they know better but that their emotions are so aroused it is hard to not use their children as pawns.

The more parents can put their animosities aside and provide cooperative parenting of their children, the better off their children will be. Every time parents are tempted to put their children in the conflict, they should remember that the children will pay an emotional price for being in that position. While parents may be satisfying their own needs, they are doing so at the emotional expense of their children. They must ask themselves if that makes it worth it. When necessary, it may be beneficial to bring in a trusted third party to consult with the two parents, provided all agree.

Q: Who should attend special occasions such as a child's birthday, school play, recital or sport's event?

Ideally, divorced parents can come to some understanding which allows them both to share in the child's special occasions without feeling that they are intruding on each other's space. If, however, there are feelings by the parents that they cannot respect each other's boundaries, then it is advisable to divide up special events by mutual agreement. For instance, one equitable solution would be that dad will attend events when they occur during dad's time with the children and mom will attend events that occur during her scheduled time with the children. In addition, many events can be celebrated twice, once with each parent. Few children have ever objected to having their birthdays celebrated twice. Perhaps the parents could rotate responsibility for giving the birthday party from year to year; mother gives the birthday party at age five and dad has responsibility for the six year birthday party. In this way, each parent can have the pleasure of planning and participating in the parties through the years. Alternate scheduling also means that the child knows what to expect each year.

A more complex situation involves once in a lifetime occasions such as graduation, receipt of special awards, a communion or a

Bar Mitzvah. In most cases both parents are proud of their child and want to participate. For these very special occasions, children are the happiest if parents will put their animosity aside in order to cooperate, at least for a day. Children have reported considerable distress if arguing and disagreements are perceived as spoiling an important event. If animosity between the parents is high, seating or circumstances should be arranged so that there can be a diplomatic minimum of interaction. Sometimes a combination of solutions may be applied, i.e., both parents attend graduation but each give a separate party for the child on different days, inviting different circles of friends and family.

Q: Under what circumstances should parents give up trying to communicate with each other?

Almost every divorced couple experiences a certain amount of very intense anger. One stage of divorce parents go through has been labeled "negative intimacy" (Ricci, 1980), in which everything that the former spouse does is experienced as irritating. It is irritating because of continued intense, negative emotional involvement with the ex-spouse. Establishing a business-type of relationship requires each parent to eventually let go of the associated anger and the intensely negative feelings for the other parent.

In most couples' experiences there is a brief period where the cessation of communication is helpful to allow dealing with hurt feelings. Each parent needs to gain a sense of "I am going to continue on now with my own existence, independently from that other person." In some instances, it is a mistake for parents to try to communicate too quickly.

As a general rule, if the period of negative intimacy continues beyond a year, parents are not healing at a reasonable enough rate to establish needed communication with each other. Some other way of problem solving should be considered. One approach that works successfully for some couples who do not communicate well is to have a shared parenting arrangement with a third party arbitrator. The arbitrator could be a mental health professional or any trusted third party who can be a tie breaker when the parents are clenched in unresolvable conflict. Usually the third party approach works better if the arbitrator is a professional person, such as a mental health or legal expert. A personal friend is more likely to be discounted if the decision is made more in one party's favor than the other's.

Obviously, it eases conflict for the children if the parents are able to communicate directly with each other. Communication is essential if there is to be shared parenting. One must make arrangements for the children to move from home to home and alert the other parent to changes in schedule, to an illness, or to a special need or circumstance. It is best to keep trying to communicate directly. Again, if this is not possible, bring in a third party. Parents who are co-parenting cannot give up trying to communicate on some level.

Q: How can mothers reconcile their own feelings about themselves when they choose to give up custody or primary residence as opposed to losing these through a judge's decision? What can they say when asked by others, "Why aren't your children living with you?" What do these women say about their choice to give up their primary parenting role?

Despite the trend towards liberation from traditional sex roles, there is little supportive sanction for a woman to relinquish her role as the children's main caretaker. Some mothers may be personally inclined to let go of the day-to-day responsibility for their children and opt to pursue career and personal interests with greater energy. Other women may feel emotionally overwhelmed, particularly immediately post-divorce. For some women, divorce means needing to go to work for the first time, possibly in a new home and community. Nevertheless, for some of these women, before they can allow dad to take over 50 percent or more of the parenting, they must first justify themselves to their own mothers, as well as other family members and friends who would find it difficult to accept a voluntary decision to relinquish a major portion of the childcare responsibility. Often a woman will opt to have an expert recommend the assignment of some responsibility for parenting to dad. Unfortunately, it is only after some of these women have had their "day in court" that society sanctions the reduction of their responsibility for full time parenting. This takes place at a great emotional cost to the woman and she may still appear to others to be a "bad mother."

Some women are able to cope well with the choice of relinquishing the primary parenting role while others are troubled by their choice. For example, one mother married very young and felt prematurely saddled with the responsibilities of motherhood. She decided, following the divorce, to establish her ex-husband's home as the primary residence of their two elementary school aged children so she could take advantage of a job offer in another part of the country. Unfortunately, this mother was tormented. She continually felt tremendous guilt and frequently expressed a great deal of anger toward her ex-husband. She could not live with her decision. She felt it was primarily her parents' reaction that was causing her emotional anguish. Unable to resolve these feelings on her own, she returned to the geographical area of the children's residence and sought psychotherapy.

This is an excruciatingly hard issue for women because most often their role as mother is part of their identity as a female. It is something which most women grow up with. In fact, until recent years, it was assumed that mothers were always to be given custody and primary residence assignments when there were divorces; children invariably stayed with the mother. It is only recently that fathers have begun to contest, and the courts with greater frequency have begun to award them custody and/or primary residence. Gardner (1977) points out that with such changing trends in recent legal decisions, some dads as well feel motivated primarily by guilt to decide to fight a legal battle for custody and primary residence. A mother's decision to give up custody usually involves a considerable change in her self-perception and her identity. It may mean that she will need some therapeutic intervention to help her to work through the difficult feelings surrounding such a change.

How does such a mother explain herself to casual contacts? Perhaps she is at a party where children are included, such as a picnic. She arrives without her children. People who know she has children ask, "Where are your children?" One mother answered by saying, "My children live with my husband because he lives in a part of town that has a far better school system." For casual social acquaintances, it is sufficient to give an accurate statement which does not reveal intimate information.

Often the hardest issue for the mothers is what to say to their own mothers and fathers. These women sometimes feel that they will be loved less by their own parents for having given up the full-time mothering of their children. Striving to please and to have the affection and respect of our own parents is a strong desire for many of us. A woman has to have a strong sense of her own needs and identity before she decides that she will relinquish being the primary parent of her children.

Q: *How can a parent know when too much is being expected of an older sibling in terms of caretaking for a younger sibling?*

In this book, ways have been discussed in which an older sibling can actually enhance a younger sibling's capacity to handle more advanced visitation at an earlier age. This means, for example, that an out-of-state or longer visitation might be possible for a younger sibling because the older sibling is along and provides some comfort and familiarity for the younger child. But there are situations in which too much can be expected of an older sibling.

Most parents desire that their children have a good sibling relationship with each other. In actuality, the most normal kind of relationship for siblings to have is an ambivalent one. In times of low stress when things are going well, siblings often express negative feelings to each other: they fight, provoke and disrupt each other. At highly stressful times, children tend to draw comfort from the fact that they have a sibling. Research (Blank & Kahn, 1982) suggests that when siblings are overly attached to each other and seem never to show signs of jealousy or resentment and never fight, these children may be overstressed and under-nurtured. Children need to have parents in their lives to take care of them. When children are not receiving enough nurturance from their parents, they will begin to take excessive care of each other. While this may be a satisfactory solution at the time, what may happen later is that these siblings will be unable to function well independently of each other. They will maintain an almost symbiotic bond. Even as adults, they may feel compelled to talk on the phone daily. Although they may marry and have children of their own, they often have very frequent contact and seem unable to ever form totally separate personalities. If you notice sibling children who never express jealousy and virtually never have conflicts with each other, it well may be that they are feeling somewhat parentally deprived and are clinging to each other.

For example, one set of preschool aged siblings of a divorced couple constantly clung to and nurtured each other. In the office they sat with their arms and legs intertwined as if it was their natural pattern to be enveloped around each other. In this case, the children had an inappropriate visitation schedule. They alternated living three months at a time with each parent. They frequently had to sever connections to the parent who had become primary. All they had of relationship continuity was each other. In this instance, major changes in the visitation schedule helped the children to maintain feelings of more continual nurturing and emotional nourishment from their parents.

Q: How should a serious illness in one parent affect visitation for children?

Parents can be loving and giving in many ways, but need to recognize their limitations. The bottom line is to be honest with yourself. If your capacity as a parent is impaired, allow your former spouse to take over more of the parenting, especially if he or she is a willing, healthy, and functioning individual. When you are rehabilitated, you can then resume more of the parenting role at that time. The children should continue to have visits with the ill parent as frequently as practical and as the youngsters request. Children should maintain visits to an ill parent as long as possible and should be allowed the opportunity to discuss their feelings, fears, and fantasies about the illness or the ill parent.

It may be important to consider how much an ill parent is able to supervise the children during visits. One divorced mother, suffering from paralysis, had a three year old daughter. This mom very much enjoyed visiting with her daughter, but could not get out of her wheelchair if, for instance, her daughter was in some kind of physical danger. In this case, a volunteer in the community took the little girl to her mother and remained nearby during the visit. Mother and daughter were still able to enjoy a wide variety of activities together. They enjoyed playing board games and cards. One of the little girl's favorite activities was to bring photographs to share with her mom.

Children need help to understand the nature of their parent's illness. Children, like adults, experience fear when confronted with uncertainty. Some parents try to deny the seriousness of an illness, or may not be aware of the repercussions of the illness themselves. They owe it to their children to make the unknown as certain as possible by finding out all they can and then addressing all of their children's questions. If there is a likelihood that the parent will die, the children must be told and helped to understand what would happen to them in that eventuality. It is difficult for parents to discuss these things, but it is necessary for the child's interests to be served.

For example, a family which consisted of a divorced mother and her seven year old daughter contacted a therapist when the girl began expressing worries about her health. Unfortunately, this mother had been diagnosed with a rare blood disease and had been told, by her physician, that the cure rate was indeterminate. This mother, like anyone confronting such tragic circumstances, had a tremendous amount of difficulty facing the fact that death was a possibility. Functioning with denial, she refused to recognize the necessity of planning for her child in the event she would not be around to parent her into adulthood. The child, so as to not speak of the forbidden, had developed personal anxieties about her own health instead.

In another family, a young mother had been diagnosed with a progressive illness which affected, amongst other functions, her vision. While she was legally blind, and had a tremendous amount of difficulty getting her daughter from place to place, her seven year old child was especially talented in dance and was involved in after-school lessons and performances. Although the dad had been actively parenting this child, the mother received strong pressure, primarily from her own parents, not to relinquish her after school caretaking role. They felt that maintaining her mothering responsibilities would help their daughter with her own rehabilitation efforts. In fact, it became an extremely negative experience for both the mother and her daughter. The girl was confused and overwhelmed by the debilitating effects of her mother's illness. Because this mother had difficulty acknowledging the limitations her illness imposed on her parenting capacity, her daughter had no permission to explore her own feelings of fear for the future and anxiety around what would happen to her. At the point therapy was initiated, the daughter had become increasingly withdrawn and socially isolated, and spoke of giving up her previous avid pursuit of performing in an effort to make it easier for her mother.

Q: What about the parent who maintains visitation begrudgingly and perhaps even hints at suspending visitation altogether?

The abandonment of a child by a parent can be a devastating

blow to the child's self-esteem. Such traumatic circumstances can result in serious interference with a child's psychological development. Therefore, in all but the most extreme cases, some degree of visitation ought to be maintained. Even in cases where the child is fearful, structured and supervised therapeutic visitation may take place toward allaying the fear. If a child is actually endangered by visiting in a parent's home, recognition of the child rather than visitation can take place. Recognition could include the sharing of gifts, phone calls, and letters. In any serious case, a mental health professional should be brought in to explore fully the reasons underlying the cessation of visitation by a parent. It is generally not in the child's best interest to sever contacts altogether.

Sometimes parents suffer from very low self-esteem, possibly from being the rejected partner in the marriage. These parents may then feel they have very little to offer their children and that the children would be better off without them. In all but the most extreme instances, this does not prove to be the case. Sometimes in dealing with their own hurt feelings, parents need to withdraw temporarily. It is advisable under such circumstances for a parent to explain to the children that he or she is hurt right now and needs to take care of him or herself. This hiatus in the relationship is certainly preferable to life-long abandonment.

Overall, children benefit from being told the truth rather than from being given excuses for a parent who terminates contact. The reasons for a parent's lack of contact are best presented as resulting from that parent's own insecurities or problems, not as the fault of the child. Children "have to be helped to appreciate that this does not mean they are unlovable, and to recognize that the defect lies in the absent parent rather than in themselves—that there is something seriously wrong with someone who cannot love his or her own child" (Gardner, 1977).

Q: What role can a step-parent play in enhancing the visitation process for children?

Step-parenting is a complex issue that continues to carry ambiguous role definitions and cultural myths. A step-family is different from a nuclear family and it takes time, often years, to integrate and form its own identity. There are many myths that have to be dispensed with and replaced with realistic expectations. One of the primary myths is that mutual affection will automatically occur between step-parent and step-child. Yet, almost without exception, the relationship between children and their natural parents is the primary affectional bond. Because of this, the best guideline for a step-parent to follow is to play a background role, especially initially, and allow the natural parent to be in charge of decision making around visitation. If the step-parent develops a close, natural attachment over time, then that may enhance the visitation experience.

Step-parents can either enhance or pose difficulty to the process of visitation depending on the role they play. Frequently, the step-parent is overly eager to become involved and this is experienced by the children as intrusive. Children especially value the opportunity to have some one-to-one time with their natural parents during their visits. Rushing too quickly into a "one big happy family" mode is a mistake. Initially a step-family is not "one big happy family"; the children know it and resent efforts to minimize the differing circumstances of each family member. It is necessary to take cues from the children themselves and move at the pace that is comfortable for them towards becoming a "blended family."

Sample Shared Parenting Agreement

Although twenty-six states currently have joint custody provisions, joint custody is not something the courts can effectively order. Research (Steinman, Zemmelman, & Knoblauch, 1985) indicates that joint custody is the most effective when agreed upon by both parents. Regardless of the legal arrangement, parents may still share parenting, as long as the court has not ordered against it. Check with your attorney for an interpretation of laws in your jurisdiction. Shared parenting, however, is not advocated for everyone. It is not for parents, one or both of whom: (1) represent a threat of physical violence; (2) have a current problem with substance abuse; (3) are showing serious emotional instability; or (4) have an inability or lack of desire to parent.

Shared parenting is for parents who have competent parenting skills and are available and willing to parent their children. The following commitments are necessary to assure that a shared parenting plan is workable:

1. Both parents are willing to make changes in the living and visitation arrangements as the developmental needs of their child change.
2. Both parents are willing to give priority to their children's needs.
3. Both parents are willing to put personal animosity aside.

The following sample parenting agreement is not a legal document but an agreement that both parents can sign to indicate good intentions and good faith in placing their child's developmental and psychological interests as primary. Obviously, a joint physical custody legal arrangement lends itself most easily to such a shared parenting plan, but one parent having sole custody does not preclude a plan that is flexibie in meeting the developmental needs of a child. Even when parents have a "joint physical custody" agreement, the specific living arrangements are not necessarily defined by the legal agreement. Therefore, all parents can benefit from a parenting agreement. The following agreement is a sample which can be modified and reproduced as needed for individual circumstances.

Sample Shared Parenting Agreement

Our primary concern is an arrangement that will enhance the psychological well being of our children following the dissolution of our marriage. It is hereby agreed that parenting of _____

_____

(children's names) will be shared as set forth below:

Residence

Option A (for parents with sole custody or joint legal custody)

1. The primary physical residence shall be in the home of

_____ (state which parent).

_____ (other parent) will have frequent and continuing contact with the children according to the following schedule: (SPECIFY SCHEDULE)

_____

_____

_____

Option B (For parents with joint physical custody)

1. Residence of the children will be alternated between parents in the following manner: (SPECIFY SCHEDULE)

_____

_____

_____

Holidays and School Vacations

2. Birthdays, special occasions, and major holidays (Christmas, New Years, President's Day, Easter, Memorial Day, The Fourth of July, Labor Day, and Thanksgiving) will be rotated according to the following schedule: (SPECIFY SCHEDULE)

_____

_____

_____

School vacations (Christmas break, spring break and summer vacation) will be shared as follows: (SPECIFY SCHEDULE)

_____

_____

_____

Major Decisions

3. Major decisions regarding education, religious training, and medical care shall be made by

_____

(state whether both parents or one only). If both parents will jointly make such decisions, then the following areas must be negotiated:

A.   Choice of school/day care
B.   Payment for school/day care, if private
C.   Access to teachers, professionals, records
D.   Medical insurance
E.   Medical treatment—choice of doctor, dentist, other professionals
F.   Payment of medical costs
G.   Religious affiliation

4. Communication with teachers, and other instructors, regarding educational progress or educational concerns will be made by

_____

(state whether one or both parents).

Maintaining Activities

5. Each parent agrees to maintain school and out of school activities during the time the children are with each of them by providing transportation and making other necessary arrangements.

Attendance at Important Events

6. Important social events and extra-curricular activities of special merit are significant to children. Therefore both parents are welcomed and encouraged to attend.

Communication

7. Communication with one parent while visiting with or residing with the other parent will be allowed via letters at all times. Phone calls will be according to the following schedule: (SPECIFY SCHEDULE; specify whether unrestricted or confined to certain time periods so as not to disrupt other activities or responsibilities)

_____

_____

_____

Modifying the Parental Agreement

8. Mother and father will confer annually about this shared parenting agreement. At a minimum of every _____ years, the above plan will be modified to take into account the changing developmental needs of _____

(children's names). If the parents are unable to concur, a professional person skilled in problem resolution, or a mediator, will be consulted and the cost of such will be paid by

_____

(specify whether both parents equally or by what proportion).

Moving

9. Neither parent (in the case of joint custody), or the parent with whom the children reside (in the case of sole custody), will move from the geographic area of

_____

without the written consent of the other parent.

Signed _____
               Mother

Signed _____
               Father

Date _____

Determining the Primary Residence

The child under five years of age needs to have a primary residence determined. This home should be with the parent who has provided the greatest proportion of caretaking activities and hours. The number of hours spent in directly meeting the needs of the child is the best indicator of who the child is likely to see as the primary source of comforting. The primary residence is, therefore, determined by identifying who has done the greatest proportion of caretaking (see Chapters One and Two).

As you read the following questions, some may seem reflective of more important child care activities than others. All represent aspects of parenting that are important sources of comfort to a child. These questions are not intended to comprise a valid or reliable test measurement but rather to serve as a guideline to assist parents in identifying those aspects of child care best relied upon to make a primary residence determination.

A possible scoring method is to write on each line the percentage of time each parent spends in each activity. Each line should total 100 percent. A sum or average of all questions can then be computed. It is best if mom and dad complete this checklist together. If that is not possible, each parent may work individually and then compare totals. If parent's answers are widely discrepant, then the evaluation of a third party professional will likely be necessary to determine the primary parent.

Checklist I consists of questions for parents of infants and toddlers, ages birth to two and one half years. Checklist II consists of questions for parents of preschool aged children, ages two and a half to five years. Parents are to complete the scale which corresponds to the age of their child. A scale should be completed for each child in the family under the age of five. For example, if there are three children under five years of age, both mother and father are to complete the scale which corresponds to the age of each child for a total of three scales completed by each parent. A total may then be computed for each child individually.

Appendix B
Checklist I
Determining the Residential Parent:
Infants and Toddlers, Ages Birth to Two and a Half Years

Percentage of Time
Spent in Activity

	Father	Mother	
100% =	_____	_____	1. Who feeds the meals to the baby?
	_____	_____	2. Who holds and comforts the baby when it cries during the day?
	_____	_____	3. Who gets up at night to hold and comfort the baby when there is crying, a bad dream, or illness?
	_____	_____	4. Who changes the baby's diapers?
	_____	_____	5. Who dresses the baby for the day?
	_____	_____	6. Who dresses the baby for bed?
	_____	_____	7. Who bathes the baby?
	_____	_____	8. Who interacts with the baby during playtime?
	_____	_____	9. Who takes the baby to the doctor when sick?
	_____	_____	10. Who takes the baby to the doctor for regular examinations?
	_____	_____	11. Who hires the babysitters?
	_____	_____	12. Who does not go to work when the baby is sick? (Only for parents who are both employed full time)
	_____	_____	13. Who introduces new foods to the baby?
	_____	_____	14. Who gives the baby vitamins?
	_____	_____	15. Who gives the baby medicine when sick?
	_____	_____	16. Who reads stories to the baby?
	_____	_____	17. Who puts the baby to bed for the night?
	_____	_____	18. Who takes the baby out in the stroller?
	_____	_____	19. Who takes the baby to day care or to the sitter's?

_____ _____ 20. Who picks up the baby from day care
                     or from the sitter's?

_____ _____ 21. Who initiates cultural and
                     enrichment activities for the baby?

_____ _____ 22. Who takes the baby to visit members
                     of the extended family?

_____ _____ TOTAL

Father   Mother

Appendix B
Checklist II
Determining the Residential Parent:
Preschool Aged Children, Ages Two and a Half to Five Years

Percentage of Time
Spent in Activity

Father	Mother	
100% = _____	_____	1. Who toilet trains the child?
_____	_____	2. Who assists the child in dressing in the morning?
_____	_____	3. Who assists the child in dressing for bed?
_____	_____	4. Who spends time working with the child to straighten up toys?
_____	_____	5. Who prepares the child's meals?
_____	_____	6. Who takes the child to social and play activities (i.e., birthday parties, zoo, park)?
_____	_____	7. Who takes the child to day care or the sitter's?
_____	_____	8. Who picks up the child from day care or the sitter's?
_____	_____	9. Who initiates conversations with the child about preschool activities and learning?
_____	_____	10. Who attends the preschool events (i.e., Holiday celebrations, special programs or parents night)?
_____	_____	11. Who spends time teaching basic skills (i.e., cutting, writing, counting)?
_____	_____	12. Who reads to the child?
_____	_____	13. Who takes the child to regularly scheduled activities (i.e., sports, cultural arts or special services such as physical or language therapy)?
_____	_____	14. Who decides how to discipline the child?
_____	_____	15. Who administers the discipline?
_____	_____	16. Who does the child call for if awake and frightened during the night?

————	————	17. Who does the child go to for comforting when physically hurt?
————	————	18. Who sees to it that the child is bathed?
————	————	19. Who plays with the child?
————	————	20. Who takes the child to the doctor when unexpectedly sick?
————	————	21. Who takes the child to the doctor for regular examinations?
————	————	22. Who determines the child care arrangements?
————	————	23. Who does not go to work when the child is sick? (Only for parents who are both employed full time.)
————	————	24. Who takes care of the child when sick?
————	————	25. Who puts the child to bed for the night?
————	————	26. Who arranges playtime with friends?
————	————	27. Who initiates cultural and enrichment activities for the child?
————	————	28. Who takes the child to visit members of the extended family?
————	————	TOTAL
Father	Mother	

Appendix C:

Maintaining Long Distance Relationships

In general, children do best when they do not have to adjust to the changes a move entails, especially when the move is long distance. If the parental divorce has occurred recently, many changes have affected the children's lives already. It is recommended that parents maintain as much constancy as possible following a divorce; therefore any move, especially a long distance move, is generally not a good idea. Even years after a divorce, a long distance move is still a difficult adjustment for children. Maintaining a relationship at a distance is exceedingly more difficult for parents as well as for children.

Children thrive on the shared experiences that take place between their parents and themselves; these are often precluded when parents and children are at a distance. The relationship between them may suffer and occasionally weaken. Consequently, long distance moves should be avoided if at all possible. Occasionally, there is no choice. Economics or personal factors may necessitate a move. Two suggestions to the parent being left behind are (1) consider whether it is possible for you to move to the new location, and (2) seek legal counsel if you feel the move is not fully warranted. There are no hard and fast rules but many judges will not give permission to move a child if in so doing a hardship situation for the child will be created. The reason for the move has to be over-riding.

Nevertheless, some such long distance moves by parents and children have been and will continue to be made. For the long distance parent we offer some suggestions for maintaining relationships.

I. Infancy to Two and a Half Years of Age
1. Send many pictures
2. Tape messages to your child in your own voice:
   a. use the child's name frequently on the tape
   b. sing children's songs
   c. tape favorite stories

3. Send little colorful, fun amusements:
    a. paper cutouts
    b. stickers
    c. autumn leaves, sea shells, whatever is found in your locale
    d. paper hats
    e. homemade items
4. Send cards at holidays and special occasions

Overall there is less that can be done for the child below age two and a half because of the lack of language and the inability of the infant to hold a memory object in mind for a long period of time. Frequent reminders that the long-distance parent exists and cares about the child are important to maintain. Phone calls are possible at the later end of this stage but the parent must not expect the child to reciprocate. Hearing the voice of the distant parent is the main goal of a call. Frequent visits are the best way to help the child up to two and a half hold the relationship in mind. Visiting may take place in both directions, depending on circumstances, with the non-residential parent traveling to the child and the parent with whom the child resides bringing the child to the other parent's location for visits.

II. Two and a Half to Five Years of Age

1. Frequent phone calls with a specific format with little expectation of reciprocity.

    Preschool aged children vary tremendously in their ability to talk on the phone. Yet, all of them love to listen. There are a number of broad principles that you can employ to make your phone calls more productive but the important thing to keep in mind is that you will carry on a one-way conversation at this age. First of all, do not ask "why" questions. Children will almost always respond, "I don't know." Second, young children cannot yet conceptualize their world in a broad sense and have a hard time responding to open-ended questions, such as "What did you do this week?" or "How are you?" Specific questions about details in their lives are the best way to get information. For example, instead of asking what your child did at school, you might ask a very specific question such as "Did you go to the playground at school this week?"

2. Send cassette tapes or letters as often as possible:
   a. personalize your messages by giving information about yourself and by using your children's names often
   b. reminisce with your child. Talk about the shared experiences you have had, such as "Remember the day we went to the zoo and you dropped your snow cone and we had to buy a new one and the monkeys were so silly."
   c. read stories onto tapes
3. Send a drawing that you have started with a request that your child finish it. Enclose a stamped, self-addressed envelope so it can be returned to you. Then talk about the experience on the phone or on one of your taped messages.
4. Insert enclosures in the letters that you send. Children love to receive little treats in the mail.
   a. stickers
   b. baseball cards
   c. balloons
   d. small pieces of candy
   e. homemade items
5. Send photographs.
6. Send a magazine subscription and get one for yourself, too. Read the stories and then share the experience long distance over the phone or on tape.

III. School-Aged Children (Six to Twelve Years Old)

Many of the techniques for the preschool-aged child are appropriate at school age as well if adapted to a higher level. Children always love to receive mail. Phone calls may take on a more conversational character with the child able to carry on a two-way conversation. Tapes can be sent in both directions with your child making them for you as well. In addition, many more ideas can be communicated because of the increased verbal skill level, such as sharing interests, hobbies, and remembering experiences over time.

1. Plan to watch the same television program and then phone to discuss it.
2. Practice reading over the phone by sending your child a reading book at his/her level and listening with your own copy in front of you.
3. Send local objects or newsclippings of interest. Encourage a collection of special remembrances that your child can keep

for himself/herself or that he/she can take to school for show and tell.

4. Send messages in nautical flags or the Russian alphabet. Send the key to deciphering the code in a separate letter or in the same letter.

5. Send magic tricks—children adore these because it makes them feel they have special skills or knowledge. They know a secret others do not.

6. Purchase some of the equipment for your children's special hobbies or interests. Things like ballet shoes, a football, the next karate belt, a backpack, or a lunch box with a special character. The idea is that you have contributed something that is an everyday or significant part of your child's life. This serves as a frequent reminder of your interest and concern.

IV. Adolescents (Twelve Years and Older)

Teenagers have reached an age where they can assume as much responsibility for traveling to visit with their non-residential parent as that parent assumes for traveling to the child's home town. However, the years from twelve to eighteen are when individual pursuits and peer relationships can surpass the importance of visiting with a parent. Therefore, in spite of their ability to do the traveling, do not be surprised if your teenagers choose not to do so. This is not necessarily a sign that the non-residential parent is not important; rather, it may be an indication of the teenager's growth away from family and towards independence. Sometimes, teenagers are totally unresponsive to efforts made by a parent to maintain a relationship across a distance. Even if this is the case, there are a number of things that can be done to let your children know that you remain interested in them and are happy to hear from them or see them when they are ready.

1. Do not call too frequently if they are not receptive but give ample permission for them to call you as often as they would like. Show them how to do this at your expense (i.e., a collect call or a credit card call). When they do call, try not to criticize or question excessively. Teenagers complain frequently about "prying."

2. Send food. Teenagers love to eat. If not food, send coupons, such as gift certificates for food or restaurants.

3. As in the case of younger children, identify your awareness of their interests and send related objects or newsclippings. Teenagers often love clothes, cosmetics, or grooming aids.

4. Most adolescents have some interest in knowing more about their heritage or roots. Send items or taped messages of interest about family background.

5. Share a magazine subscription in a subject of interest— skiing, racquetball, dancing, skating.

6. Arrange to purchase tickets to a local athletic or musical event and send them.

References

Blank, S. P., & Kahn, M. D. (1982). *The Sibling Bond.* New York: Basic Books.

Blos, P. (1979). *The Adolescent Passage.* New York: International Universities Press.

Brazelton, T. B. (1984, September 5). *Rocky Mountain News.* Children under stress. (1986, October 27). U.S. News and World Report.

Emde, R. N., Gaensbauer, T. J., & Harmon, R. J. (1976). *Emotional Expression in Infancy.* New York: International Universities Press.

Gardner, R. A. (1977). *The Parents Book About Divorce.* New York: Doubleday & Co., Inc.

Guidubaldi, J., Cleminshaw, H. D., Perry, J. D., & McLoughin, C. S. (1983). The impact of parental divorce on children: Report of the nationwide NASP study. *School Psychology Review,* 12:300-323.

Hetherington, E. M. (1972). Effects of father absence on personality development of adolescent girls. *Developmental Psychology,* 1(3):313-326.

Kalter, N. (1977). Children of divorce in an outpatient psychiatric population. *American Journal of Orthopsychiatry,* 47(1):40-51.

Kalter, N., Riemer, B., Brickman, A., and Chen, J. W. (1985). Implications of parental divorce for female development. *Journal of the American Academy of Child Psychiatry,* 24(5):538-544.

Kaplan, L. (1978). *Oneness and Separateness: From Infant to Individual.* New York: Simon and Schuster.

Kelly, J. B., & Wallerstein, J. S. (1976). The effects of parental divorce: Experiences of the child in early latency. *American Journal of Orthopsychiatry,* 76(1):20-32.

Mahler, M. (1979). *The Selected Papers of Margaret Mahler,* Vol. II. New York: Jason Aronson.

Ricci, I. (1980). *Mom's House, Dad's House.* New York: Collier Books.

Shinn, M. (1978). Father absence and children's cognitive abilities. *Psychological Bulletin,* 85:295-324.

Sorosky, A. D. (1977). The psychological effects of divorce on adolescents. *Adolescence,* 12(45):123-136.

Spitz, R., & Wolf, M. (1946). Anaclitic depression, an inquiry into the genesis of psychiatric conditions in early childhood, II. *The Psychoanalytic Study of the Child,* 2:313-342.

Steinman, S., Zemmelman, S., & Knoblauch, T. (1985). A study of parents who sought joint custody following divorce: Who reaches agreement and sustains joint custody and who returns to court. *Journal of the American Academy of Child Psychiatry,* 24(5):554-562.

Stern, D. N. (1985). *The Interpersonal World of the Infant.* New York: Basic Books.

Wallerstein, J. S. (1983, September 10). Children of divorce: Findings from a ten year study; Parent-child relationships following divorce. Presentation at the Interdisciplinary Committee in Child Custody Annual Conference, Keystone, Colorado.

Wallerstein, J. S. (1985). Children of divorce: Preliminary report of a ten-year follow-up of older children and adolescents. *Journal of the American Academy of Child Psychiatry,* 24(5): 545-553.

Wallerstein, J. S., & Kelly, J. B. (1974). The effects of parental divorce: The adolescent experience. In E. J. Anthony & C. Koupernik (Eds.), *The Child in His Family.* New York: Wiley and Sons.

Wallerstein, J. S., & Kelly, J. B. (1975). The effects of parental divorce: Experiences of the preschool child. *Journal of the American Academy of Child Psychiatry,* 14:600-616.

Wallerstein, J. S., & Kelly, J. B. (1980). *Surviving the Breakup: How Children and Parents Cope with Divorce.* New York: Basic Books.

Mitch Baris, Ph.D., has practiced psychology in the Boulder and Denver, Colorado communities for the past fifteen years. The main focus of his work has been psychotherapy with children, adolescents, and adults. He has functioned as a custody mediator, a member of a child custody evaluation team, and has been involved in adversarial court proceedings as an expert witness. Working with families to determine custody and to resolve the difficulties following divorce, Mitch has had first-hand experience observing the impact of divorce conflict on families.

Carla Garrity, Ph.D., practices child psychology in Denver, Colorado. She helped start the Neuro Development Center, a multidisciplinary team for the assessment and treatment of children. For the past eleven years, she has also taught child psychopathology at the University of Denver's School of Professional Psychology. Her special interest in infants and pre-school aged children has often brought her into the courtroom as an expert witness and into the family arena as a mediator for visitation planning.

This book evolved from Mitch's and Carla's work as they became increasingly interested in finding a means to help families resolve residence and visitation issues outside the courtroom.